WARNING:
Only to be read if ordinary is no longer OK!

help@corporatedenial.com

Clear direction?	Inaction?
Rapid response?	Lost purpose?
Tight focus?	Painful waste?
Powerful communication?	Confusion?
Energetic workforce?	Muddled communication?
Confident management?	Energy loss?
Vibrant teamwork?	Meaningless corporate values?
Talent magnet?	Low corporate libido?
Amazing relationships?	Corporate Denial?

What do you recognize?

Need help?

help@corporatedenial.com

Corporate Denial

Confronting the world's most
damaging business taboo

Will Murray

wjm

First published 2004 by
Capstone Publishing Limited (a Wiley Company)
The Atrium
Southern Gate
Chichester
West Sussex
PO19 8SQ
www.wileyeurope.com
E-mail (for orders and customer service enquires): cs-books@wiley.co.uk

CIP catalogue records for this book are available from the British Library and the US Library of Congress

ISBN 184112611X

Typeset in 11/14pt Palatino by Sparks, Oxford – www.sparks.co.uk
Printed and bound in Great Britain by TJ International Ltd, Padstow, Cornwall
This book is printed on acid-free paper responsibly manufactured from sustainable forestry in which at least
two trees are planted for each one used for paper production.

To Annie
For the love of a good woman!
I love you for just being yourself.

To George and Henry
I love you not only for who you are but
for who I am when I am with you.
Believe in each other
See everything there is to see
Keep faith with God
Be the best you can be.

To Mum and Dad
Thank you for your unceasing support and helping
me to understand the importance of families.

Corporate Stress kills!

Our research has shown that:

- more than 40% of large and medium-sized UK organizations fail to communicate properly to their staff;
- in 40% of large and medium-sized UK organizations, managers don't listen to each other;
- one third of organizations say one thing and do another;
- almost one in three organizations suffer from continual reorganization; and
- one in five organizations won't take tough decisions.

Published information shows that:

- managers are generally working one month a year longer than they were 20 years ago;
- stress-related claims have soared twelve-fold; 6000 cases are waiting to go through the courts at any one time;
- 13 million working days are lost to stress each year in the UK alone;
- 200 million working days are lost a year in the US; and
- Corporate Stress is costing western companies hundreds of billions of dollars!

Is it time to become a Corporate Stress buster?

Is it time to confront Denial?

Will Murray

Recently described as 'the Dr Ruth of organizations', Will Murray is an organizational coach and relationship troubleshooter with a difference.

A leading exponent in organizational effectiveness, Will lifts the lid on the power of relationships to determine an organization's future, bringing a whole new meaning to the term 'relationship management'.

When he left university, he cut his commercial teeth in the fast-moving world of retail buying, working for organizations such as the Dixons Group, House of Fraser and Debenhams, where he quickly learnt the importance of both tight organizational focus and strong relationships.

Taking his career in a new direction, Will was given the opportunity to apply his hard-learnt trader's savvy to the highfalutin world of corporate life, where he pioneered sector marketing and relationship selling for BT and later Ernst & Young.

Recognizing that the ideas behind these concepts were as essential throughout organizations as they were at the customer interface, Will used them to challenge the status quo on how whole organizations should be structured and motivated to help them succeed and grow.

Inspired by the world-changing events in countries such as South Africa and the former Yugoslavia, he has adapted approaches used to resolve deep-rooted cultural conflicts to work in the corporate environment.

Will has also recognized the potential of adapting approaches proven in the fields of personal and relationship development. Long overlooked in an organizational context, he found that the ideas behind relationship counselling soon proved their worth in a commercial setting.

Sometimes referred to as 'marriage guidance for companies', Will is using exciting and innovative cutting edge ideas such as Truth and Reconciliation in Business and Relationship Mapping to transform the market prospects of all manner of organizations, from schools to power companies.

Already the author of *Brand Storm*, a tale of consumer passion, betrayal and revenge, and *Hey You!*, introducing the art of explosive thinking, Will has also worked in a variety of leading creative agencies as diverse as Brand House, tgd and The Fourth Room, and now helps organizations from major PLCs down to small independents to build amazingly powerful business relationships.

will@willjmurray.com

Contents

Acknowledgements

Annalese Banbury

The ability of Annalese to get straight to the heart of an issue has been invaluable in crafting *Corporate Denial*. She possesses some of the most intuitive people skills of anyone I have ever worked with and has applied them tirelessly in the development of this book. Thank you!

David Birt

For several years David has been inspirational, funny, challenging and a consistent source of encouragement and support. Since we first met we have shared ideas and built on each other's thoughts, and without David, *Corporate Denial* would not be the book it now is. Thank you!

Tim Guy

Tim is one of those rare people who can see an idea while it is still a shapeless mist and then have the courage of his convictions to act on it. He has been an immense support and instrumental in developing these ideas. Thank you!

Lauris Calnan

Few people know more about the habits and foibles of organizations than Lauris. As a corporate research expert, Lauris's insight into the behaviour and thought patterns of companies has been a constant check and balance to our ideas. Thank you!

Richard Burton

Richard was one of the first to recognize the potential of this book and as a founder of Capstone, Richard's expert eye for a good idea has helped us to fast-track the production of *Corporate Denial*. Thank you!

John Moseley

In his capacity as an editor, John has helped us to develop our ideas and made *Corporate Denial* the book it now is. Thank you!

Jonathan Ball

The fact that Jonathan was one of the co-founders of the Eden Project comes as no surprise to me. His passion for innovation and obvious excitement about new ideas always make Jonathan fun and challenging to work with. He manages to see things that others can't and his critical approach and analysis have been a great help in preparing this book. Thank you!

Eric Dinsey

Eric is an expert in customer service and I highly value his opinion. Eric has been a great sounding board for ideas for several years now. Thank you!

The team at Wiley

Writing a book is very much a team effort and working with Ian, Scott, Jenny and the rest of the team at Wiley has transformed the production of *Corporate Denial* from hard graft into an enjoyable and rewarding challenge. Thank you!

Foreword

Stop, look and listen ...

The forces of history are at work and we can now rip up the rule book that served society through the 20th century. In our world of frightening uncertainty there have never been greater challenges faced nor a greater divide between our hopes for the future and their fulfilment. The new magnetic field and force of world politics, a world with national governments no longer in control, distorts the compass point. We know we are all global citizens but we are no longer sure about the direction of due north.

Goodbye industrial economy, hello global knowledge economy. Goodbye the state running things, hello Global Joe Citizen empowered by the technology-driven changes in the first years of the 21st century and with a mobility beyond the wildest dreams of those who brought us into this world. Yes, I do mean us, fellow global citizens.

The 20th century was all about us having to rely on governments to deal with those issues beyond our personal capacity to influence, regardless of how much concern and anxiety were personally invested. Simply put, this has all changed.

Just as the world landscape is now determined by a new order of collaborative arrangements, so the time has come for us all to seize control of our choices and pursue new personal values-led collaborations. That great humanitarian Mahatma Gandhi captures it in his timeless wisdom: 'you must be the change that you wish to see in the world.'

In order for the world to work for me, I have to make it work for you. Together you and I must make it work for all our fellow global citizens, not least the 800 million who will go to bed hungry tonight. If the values, beliefs, ideals and ethics that we take with us to work each day do not result in our business environment adding rather than detracting from the sum of global co-operation, our long-term personal and corporate business goals are doomed to failure.

But what we do have is a business environment pregnant with possibility and unfettered by past constraints of geography or technology. It is up to us as individuals to nurture an atmosphere where values-led decision-making thrives.

Corporate culture looking beyond traditional business horizons is the agenda item of the moment. The public scrutiny and disapprobation flowing from corporate scandals on a global scale request and require a re-evaluation of compliance with ethical, environmental and social imperatives. A new collective, caring culture is no longer just an attitude of mind rather than depth of pocket; it makes good business sense.

Therein is your desirable future: you are the engine that drives the new connection between global business and your community. Integrity is the fuel that drives both the engine and the process. Take control of your choices and root them in the eternal triangle of truth, trust and peace. Without truth there can be no trust and without trust there can be no peace. Adopt this landscape for mapping your relationships. Until people trust you, they will not change with you. So many of today's leaders now fail to fulfil their ambitions for this very reason. Remember, Gandhi's immense power flowed simply from exercising his values.

Never underestimate the power of good intent. When you change, the world changes with you. Think about it: by the very fact that you have picked up this book, you are positively investing now in the sort of future you wish to have and wish to see for your children. I ask you to look at Will Murray's book with eyes that see tomorrow differently. After all, this is exactly what Will is doing in writing this book for his children, George and Henry.

The more your ambitions are aligned to the benefit of humanity as well as your business, the more relevant the product of your labour will be. In turn, the more valuable you become in the market place, the greater your capacity to take control of your choices and your future. And please remember this: a values-led approach and entrepreneurial spirit advancing an enterprise culture are not mutually exclusive.

The lesson I learnt above all others in co-founding and making the Eden Project happen was that there is nothing more powerful in this world than an idea whose time has come. Eden's international acclaim has grown from its ability to chime with Global Joe's concerns and aspirations for the future. Its spectacle comes from nature working with mankind's technological expression in a new order of collaboration. It is relevant. It sends signals to the world. It connects with global issues and takes ownership of part of the sustainable future debate.

On the distant future day you finally retire from your business world, your peers, looking back, will judge you on your actions and achievements, not just on your beliefs. Think of Will's book as an organizational framework and focus for your ideas for tomorrow. Use it as a compass pointing you in the direction of those personal and business priorities you need to revisit in order to deliver your desirable future.

Jonathan Ball MBE
Sunny Cornwall

Preface

The ideas in *Corporate Denial* are based on over 20 years of observing the way that organizations behave. Some of this time has been spent working for major organizations in various roles, from rookie corporate trainee through to senior executive. Some has been spent working in and amongst small business organizations. The rest of the time has either been spent helping organizations as an organizational coach and relationship troubleshooter or trying to deal with them as a customer.

Throughout this time, I have been driven by a fundamental interest in people, in their relationships, in the way they communicate and in the way they behave together as groups and in organizations.

To put *Corporate Denial* into perspective, let me explain where I'm coming from: why I have written it and why I believe it is different from other books you may have read.

The ideas in the book started to come together late one evening at the Greenbank Hotel in Falmouth, Cornwall, overlooking the Fal Estuary.

After a long day facilitating a workshop with my colleagues David Birt and Annalese Banbury, we were relaxing in the lounge and contemplating the experiences of the day. Eventually we got round to the questions:

Why, in a world where business training and advice abound, does the performance of all types of organizations still vary from the sublime to the ridiculous?

Why were people that we knew were good managers struggling on, frustrated and worn down working in poor organizations?

Desperately trying not to descend into a rant, we still couldn't stop ourselves getting angry.

Why were so many companies so awful?

Why was the service we experienced as customers often so poor?

Why were companies failing to build effective long-term relationships?

Why were some people so hard to help?

Why did so few organizations amaze us?

And why did so many organizations seem to get away with it?

Maybe we were influenced by our environment – the Greenbank Hotel being famous as the location where *The Wind in the Willows* was written – or maybe it was the wine, but as the evening progressed, the mists began to rise and we started to recognize the importance of some fundamental truths. These truths started to form a pattern based on the types of relationship that different organizations develop.

Since that evening I have researched, developed and tested the picture that emerged to the point that it is now the foundation of this book. The stark message is that many businesses today are systematically failing to reach their full potential, but the good news is that there are ways to deal with it.

I am not saying that companies can't or don't succeed; rather that the culture governing the way many of them think and behave is inevitably limiting their long-term success.

I believe that the condition I describe as 'Corporate Denial' is endemic in many businesses and that everybody – directors, employees, shareholders, customers and the greater community as a whole – suffers as a result.

I believe there are certain patterns of behaviour that most amazingly successful organizations naturally exhibit, thus immunizing themselves from the dangers of Corporate Denial.

These patterns of behaviour can be learnt and adopted by organizations correctly motivated to do so. I will introduce a series of 'Maps', or approaches, that can help organizations build stronger relationships and become more successful.

Writing this book is the culmination of everything I have done in my business life to date. I have always refused to accept things as they are simply because that is the way they have always been or because I held a minority view.

I believe in trying to do what is right, not purely from a moral point of view – although that comes into it – but from the perspective that it makes us more effective and ultimately delivers greater success. This has always been my approach, even when at times it became clear that I was endangering any immediate prospects of success or reward.

This is what drove me to leave the corporate stronghold of BT, where I worked for ten years. It is also what drove me out of the arms of Ernst & Young, another bastion of corporate life.

If I had been more accepting by nature and had wanted less of a challenge, – if I had been more willing to accept ordinary as OK – I might still have been working for one of these companies or somewhere similar, as many of my ex-colleagues still are.

But I chose a different route: to become an independent organizational coach and relationship troubleshooter, bold enough to hang on to my core beliefs and practise what I preach.

With the consistent goal of helping organizations develop excellent and successful relationships I have seen it as my responsibility, rightly or wrongly, to challenge both client thinking and behaviour. I challenge not only my clients' approach to relationships, communication and organizational ideas, but also – in an effort to make them the very best they could be – question their personal behaviour and search for a personal demonstration of stated beliefs and principles.

I have been fortunate to meet people along the way, such as David Birt, Tim Guy and Annalese Banbury, who have shared my vision for how businesses should be run. Working together we have developed many of the principles behind this book and often shared the task of helping clients grow.

Having friends and colleagues such as this has made a major difference to me personally and given me the strength to persevere.

It has been a roller-coaster ride – but what a ride! The last few years have provided me with the opportunity to become involved with a variety of people in a whole host of different organizations facing a myriad of different opportunities, and I genuinely believe that I have stuck to my guns and consistently challenged people hard – even when it has been uncomfortable.

I have applied the belief that every aspect of an organization's behaviour and communication should be driven by a common set of principles, and my approach to organizations usually takes four essential stages:

- purpose – being totally clear about what is to be achieved, ensuring that there is full agreement on this amongst the leadership team and that they can all explain it simply but powerfully to others;
- focus – making sure that all of the organization's energy is focused on that agreed purpose;
- relationships – developing solid internal and external relationships as the core of the organization's market differentiation and success; and
- communication – ensuring that the organization's internal communication is totally effective, meaningful and focused, and that external communication is consistent with the organization's goals and culture, and is supported by demonstrable benefits.

In some respects my role has resembled that of a butler in the Victorian era. I have seen companies in their raw undisguised state in the morning, without make-up, unshaven and sometimes even worse. I have witnessed the arguing and making up, been privy to intimate secrets, cleaned up mess, and ultimately been charged with making clients look the part when they were ready to entertain the world.

The intensity and intimacy of the relationships that I have been able to enjoy with clients has given me a unique insight into the complex world of organizational leadership, business relationships and corporate culture, and has helped me to understand why some companies continue to succeed and others go off the boil.

Working with companies from the inside out, challenging them to personally demonstrate their core principles, communicate better internally, create stronger cultures and relationships and back up their market messages with proof and evidence, has become a way of life.

I have put the spotlight firmly on agreed business principles and goals, defining standards of behaviour, proof, evidence and demonstration – and it has not always made me popular!

Making 'challenge' a way of life wins you some good friends and makes you a few, if not enemies, shall we say 'detractors'?

Being asked to justify why they want to do something has been a welcome revelation to some, but an unwelcome, rather impertinent intrusion to others.

Some people don't want their decisions questioned, some are embarrassed because they don't have the answers and some are afraid to question senior directors' wishes. Others openly admit that they don't think anyone has the answers but think that doing anything is better than doing nothing at all. ('After all, we've got the budget and if I don't spend it this year then I won't get it again next year …!')

I have seen glass ceilings – not to people's careers, but on the ability of people to question and challenge decision-making and decision-making criteria. I have also seen glass walls and floors, with people unwilling or unprepared to involve their peers or those that work for them in their thinking.

There is nothing like getting into the lifeblood of an organization without actually being part of it to open your eyes. It's like being an old family friend: you are close but not actually family, which allows you to be slightly more objective when viewing the goings-on around you.

By rolling up my sleeves and getting stuck in, I get to know individuals across every function and every level of a business. My experience has been that as long as you are not perceived to be a threat but as someone trying to help, people can't be more open or keen to contribute. This has played a key part in allowing me to 'reality check' the ideas in this book.

But going back to the Greenbank Hotel: a picture emerged that evening that has become the core of our philosophy and a cornerstone of confronting Corporate Denial.

The problems in many of the organizations that I have worked with were endemic in the way they were set up. Organizational culture was seen as less mission-critical than other aspects of organizational infrastructure, such as sales, production or setting up IT and finance systems.

Unfortunately, unlike individuals, organizations have no natural inbuilt change mechanisms, and organizational culture very quickly determines the outcome of future relationships. For many organizations, redefining and changing even a newly created culture is beyond them.

These issues are made worse when an organization is on its third or fourth management team and the overall culture dissolves into a series of personality cults driven by separate individuals within the organization.

Corporate Denial addresses these issues. It captures as accurately as possible the best things that I have seen achieved and identifies hurdles that exist to be overcome. It examines why some organizations grasp greatness whilst others actively seem to turn their back on it.

Every situation, every gem and every flaw described in *Corporate Denial* is based on real-life experience. You will find simple solutions based on approaches that I have implemented successfully with clients and the things that I have seen successful clients do naturally.

As the book progresses I will:

- describe life in an organization suffering Corporate Stress, introduce the concept of Corporate Denial, talk about the symptoms of Corporate Denial including the etiquette of inaction and explain how to diagnose its existence;
- summarize the established principles of personal effectiveness and show how these principles effect organizations;
- highlight the importance of working culture and show how no organization can ever totally succeed without understanding the power of culture to determine long-term success;
- introduce the concept of corporate evolution, with Primitive Organizations at one end of the corporate spectrum and Advanced Organizations at the other, and explain why some organizations grow up but others never do;

- bring to life the concept of 'Truth and Reconciliation in Business' and show how this process is the only way for some organizations to break free from Corporate Denial;
- explain how to become an amazingly successful organization through the application of 'Relationship Mapping'; how using Truth, Culture, Message and Behaviour Maps can help you master your own destiny, stop OK from ever being OK and create a culture that will help you become the very best you can be; and
- share my belief in applying the art of theatre to business and draw attention to the importance of Active Constitutions and Corporate Ritual in uniting a whole organization.

You will be challenged to face up to life, not as you see it but through the eyes of your employees, colleagues and customers, and maybe face some harsh realities.

- Is your organization Primitive, Mercenary, Feudal or Advanced?
- Do your relationships need rescuing?
- Could your organization be suffering from Corporate Denial?

You may be shocked, you may disagree with parts of it; in fact, I am the first to admit that *Corporate Denial* is very challenging in places. When I first tested the ideas, some people reacted so strongly to the picture we described that they refused to accept its existence.

Is this Denial in action?

Are you in Denial?

You decide.

will@willjmurray.com

The Seven Sins of Denial

Undeniable evidence

wjm

Collecting the evidence

Knowing something is one thing; being able to prove it is quite another.

Twenty-plus years of working with organizations gives you a pretty good feel for what organizational life is like – but what if my experiences were atypical?

To put my mind at rest I decided to research the market. I commissioned some independent research from Lauris Calnan at the Bingham Calnan Group. We researched the opinions of over a thousand UK companies, ranging from those with less than 50 employees to enterprise organizations with between 50 and 200 employees, to larger companies with over 200 employees.

We needed to find out whether Corporate Denial was fact or fiction!

Focusing on some of the most damaging symptoms of Corporate Denial we asked whether their organization experienced any of the following:

- poor internal communication;
- managers not listening to each other;
- an unwillingness to take tough decisions;
- continual reorganization;
- looking inward;
- saying one thing and doing another; and
- ineffective reward and recognition.

The answers were very revealing!

Overall findings

The top-level findings are clear for all to see.

The seven sins of Denial – all organizations

Percentage of organizations that admitted to:

1	Poor communication	31%
2	Managers not listening to each other	30%
3	Saying one thing and doing another	23%
4	Continual reorganization	22%
5	Ineffective reward and recognition	22%
6	Unwillingness to take tough decisions	16%
7	Looking inward	10%

Top of the list are two of the prime causes of Corporate Denial – poor internal communication and managers not listening to each other. Almost one-third of companies are suffering these debilitating problems.

Nearly one in four companies says one thing and does another, continually reorganizes and fails to reward performance properly.

Based on this sample, the scale of Corporate Denial starts to become clear. This may only be the view of a thousand organizations, but it must provide a pretty good indication of what is happening right across business.

And if the overall picture gives cause for concern, the picture for larger organizations provides even more reasons to worry.

Enterprise organizations

The seven sins of Denial – enterprise organizations, 50–199 employees

Percentage of organizations that admitted to:

1	Poor communication	43%
2	Managers not listening to each other	40%
3	Saying one thing and doing another	33%
4	Continual reorganization	32%
5	Ineffective reward and recognition	29%
6	Unwillingness to take tough decisions	21%
7	Looking inward	15%

Poor communication and failure to listen top the list again and are present in 43% and 40% respectively of organizations of this size!

Constant reorganization is affecting almost one in three organizations and lack of integrity – the result of saying one thing and doing another – is even more common.

One in five will not take a tough decision.

The saving grace is that only 15% are looking inward, which provides hope for customers.

Larger organizations

The seven sins of Denial – organizations of over 200 employees

When we look at the largest organizations, the situation is just as worrying but the order of the sins changes somewhat.

Poor internal communication and the refusal of managers to listen to each other remain the most common symptoms of Denial, again at 43% and 40% respectively.

As might be expected, the larger the organization becomes, the more the problems of continual reorganization increase, making it the third most common symptom. Also rising up the list are looking inward and ineffective reward and recognition. This possibly reflects the greater scope for looking inward in a larger organization and the increased problems in recognizing those who are adding value and those who are along for the ride.

Saying one thing and doing another becomes less of an issue, maybe reflecting the number of people who can record what was said in the first place.

Also dropping down the list is the unwillingness to take tough decisions. Perhaps the larger the organization, the less personal it becomes and the more people feel able to cope with tough decisions.

Assessing the impact of the sins of Denial

We asked those who recognized each problem how much it was affecting the performance of their organization. The results were frightening.

Percentage of organizations that said there was a dramatic or significant impact on overall organizational effectiveness:

1	Ineffective reward and recognition	42%
2	Continual reorganization	36%
3	Unwillingness to take tough decisions	32%
4	Looking inward	32%
5	Managers not listening to each other	29%
6	Poor communication	27%
7	Saying one thing and doing another	27%

Where there is evidence of at least one symptom of Denial within an organization, it is highly likely that there will be more.

If one symptom has a dramatic or significant effect on organizational performance, what effect will multiple symptoms have?

No denying it

The results of this independent survey back up my own experience: Corporate Denial is out there amongst organizations of all sizes.

It might at first glance be easy to say that Corporate Denial is affecting larger organizations more than smaller ones, but I am not sure that this tells the whole story.

When you think that even in organizations of less than 50 employees almost one in three is already experiencing problems with internal communication and listening to each other, and that more than a fifth are constantly reorganizing, you have to ask yourself what is going wrong.

These organizations should not be suffering in this way at this stage in their evolution and growth.

In large organizations, a whopping 40% have stopped communicating properly and are no longer listening to each other's view. No wonder relationships are suffering badly and Corporate Denial has become the world's most damaging business taboo.

So what exactly is going on?

Affected by these issues?

E-mail us at help@corporatedenial.com.

1.0 Corporate Stress

The road to Corporate Denial

wjm

Let's be honest!

Are you still searching for excellence? Are you confused as to whether your business should be funky, whether you need a corporate witch doctor or whether your cheese is going stale?

Do you ever ask yourself the following?

- 'Why with so many business books, training courses, MBAs and management theories isn't every leadership team in the world already running an amazingly successful organization?'
- 'Why are so many of the people I interact with on a daily basis working for unremarkable, obviously flawed and pretty average organizations?'
- 'Why doesn't recruiting highly effective people into an organization guarantee amazing success?'

I have regularly asked myself these questions and now recognize that in a world where fad and fashion are becoming ever more common, the only way to go is to revert to tried and tested common sense and basic principles.

Throughout the years I have spent working with and for various organizations, I have never ceased to be amazed at the enormous variety of approach and attitude that different people have exhibited, and the intriguing – and, at first glance, apparently unpredictable – relationship between competence and success.

I now believe the key to the success of a number of businesses can be put down to accidents of history, geography and, dare I say it, plain good luck.

The survival and in some cases success of these organizations can be put down to good foresight followed by good fortune rather than good management. For example:

- getting hold of a good basic product to sell;
- being in the right place at the right time;
- offering slightly better value than competitors;
- having customers that have nowhere else to go;
- having customers without enough knowledge, energy or interest to take action; and
- being protected from competition by some type of regulations or natural monopoly.

You might argue with this, saying, 'Yes, but isn't it funny, the harder I work the luckier I get?'

What I call chance you might describe as hard graft, risk-taking and good judgement, and you may be right.

But is it your hard work, risk-taking and good judgement, or are you the lucky recipient of a legacy left over from previous years?

Do you simply have a product that is in demand regardless of who is selling it?

Let's face it:

Thousands of companies are well run, hard working, focused on their customers and doing very well, thank you. I have worked with some of them and they are inspirational.

Thousands of companies are well run, hard working and focused on their customers, but are still learning crucial lessons, building vital relationships or struggling in highly competitive, fast-moving market places and are yet to fully enjoy the fruits of their labour. I have worked with some of these as well and their grit and determination is *truly* inspirational.

Yet thousands of businesses today are either still enjoying the legacy of past hard work and success or are, for one of several reasons, protected from any type of significant competition. They may or may not still have the same management team that led them to success but now succeed despite themselves.

They lack focus and many have lost the spirit that created their original success. They waste money, argue amongst themselves, have a tendency to be self-indulgent, react very badly to challenge and, even if they are not actually bad as a business, miss out on the opportunity to use their past success as a springboard to what could be a great future for all involved, including customers and employees.

These businesses have neither the immediate reason nor the desire to perform to their maximum. They are focused on making enough money to satisfy the needs of the management team, the expectations of shareholders and the demands of employees. These organizations are in limbo and I believe that they are widespread in business today.

When I started to think about businesses being in limbo I got the dictionary out to check the exact meaning of the word and it is quite interesting. There are, as you might expect, several meanings, but most relate to exclusion, neglect, confinement, uncertainty, being kept waiting and denial of ultimate reward – which sums up some organizations I know pretty well!

The individuals that condemn their organizations to corporate limbo are not necessarily out-and-out bad, but they are certainly not good either. Many of their customers, employees, managers, shareholders and even the executives themselves are often left feeling excluded, uncertain and disappointed as a result of the whole experience.

As you may have guessed, these organizations frustrate the hell out of me: they have significant resources available to them but waste them in apparent irresponsibility.

> **These organizations are suffering Corporate Stress!**

What is Corporate Stress?

Corporate Stress affects organizations in a similar manner to the way human conditions affect human beings and there are identifiable factors that increase the propensity of an organization to suffer from it.

Good living seems to be a major contributing factor for organizations as it is for people. Putting on too much weight, not exercising, worrying too much and advancing years all dull the appetite of an organization for hard work and unstinting service.

A key cause of stress in humans is a feeling that issues in our life are escalating to a point that we begin to feel out of control. We feel we are being pulled in an ever-increasing number of directions and eventually we stop viewing life in a rational way.

Our ability to cope with even simple tasks is dramatically reduced to the point that everything we attempt to do becomes markedly less effective and eventually appears unmanageable. This is similar to what happens when an organization is in the throes of Corporate Stress.

Corporate Stress and subsequently Corporate Denial are brought on when an organization lacks focus, tries to achieve conflicting goals, is doing the wrong things, lacks motivation or is trying to do too many different things.

Any organization so caught up in the daily running of its business that it neglects to attend to its ongoing health is susceptible to Corporate Stress.

It is easy for an organization to neglect the things that guarantee its long-term health. These things are *vital* to ongoing success but are never as *time-critical* as short term deadlines – hence the problem.

Corporate Stress can be triggered by too much success or – even worse for the health of the organization – by too much success too easily achieved! This invariably seems to lead to contradictory and unhelpful distractions for both the organization as a whole and its most important individuals.

The other major cause of Corporate Stress besides lack of focus is lack of integrity.

As soon as you stop trying to ensure that every aspect of your organization from strategy through service delivery to customer service is telling the same story, Corporate Stress becomes unavoidable.

So what happens in a stressed-out organization?

Why when some managers always try and do the right things ... do others behave in an insane way?

Talking to a group of business people the other day, I was surprised by the reaction to something I said. I had asked a question about why some people leave part of themselves behind when they go to work and why those people do things at work that they would never dream of doing at home and vice versa.

A member of the audience stood up and stated that they thought it was inconceivable that anyone would behave the same at work as they do at home.

To me this highlighted a major issue.

I believe that one of the core reasons for the success of truly great organizations is their ability to firstly recruit and secondly encourage people to do this very thing: to treat others in the organization and the organizations' resources with the same respect they treat their own friends, family and property.

Admittedly aligning personal and corporate values is not always essential to success: we all know of organizations staffed by accomplished actors that do very well, thank you. However, not to recognize that this is at least something to strive for is, I think, a sad state of affairs.

With the length of time each of us remains working in the same job decreasing all the time, it is very easy for even the most talented and dedicated of us to start treating life at work as if it was a virtual reality video game.

> **When things go wrong we can press
> the escape button and start another game!**

A sense of unreality can overtake common sense and lead at best to lazy thinking and at worst to antisocial behaviour to the detriment of the whole organization.

I have certainly seen directors of big PLCs as well as teams charged with running government departments behave this way, and the people who lose out are the shareholders or taxpayers who pick up the bill!

Why do some have the courage to speak out … whilst others say nothing?

When I first left college and started work, this took some getting used to. As a bright-eyed and bushy-tailed young manager fresh from my studies, I at first refused to believe the stories bandied around by more experienced colleagues about the way my betters behaved.

Surely no-one could behave in the way I was reliably informed that they did. 'What about integrity and honour?' I gasped, to the merriment of my older, wiser friends. But in time I came to learn that 'hear no evil, see no evil, speak no evil' really is the code of practice for many senior and middle managers.

When I work with individuals who dare to speak out and who create an environment where others are encouraged to do the same, the power is awesome.

I once worked in an organization with two separate sales divisions. One division operated the old 'don't you dare say that' approach, whilst the other division was more open and prepared to listen to news both good and bad.

The difference in culture and performance was dramatic but the most obvious difference was in where the talent in the organization migrated to.

Good people – the ones we need on board when we want to become amazingly successful – love to work where they can express honest opinions and, when necessary, tell the truth about the emperor and his new clothes!

The sad truth is that a willingness to speak out is still quite rare in some companies and that the more senior people become, the more they have to lose and the more likely they are to say nothing.

Watching people skirt around the truth has been informative; I have come to recognize what I now call the 'etiquette of inaction'. As in any other club, directors and senior managers have an implicit code of conduct that governs relationships and has to be learnt when you join the board. Adhering to the code is what helps them avoid treading on each other's toes.

Since I discovered the etiquette of inaction I have been able to understand corporate behaviour a lot more clearly. It is easy to see why organizations, where the etiquette of inaction is alive and well, never become amazingly successful.

Why when some managers are desperate to learn ... are others still into shooting messengers?'

Many organizations, even in this day and age, still hate hearing bad news. This is driven by their attitude to learning: at heart, organizations are either learning organizations or they are not.

Those that are not learning organizations genuinely hate bad news. They shoot messengers and prefer to bury their head in the sand till they get kicked out of their complacency and forced to act. Fortunately (or not) for some of them, they have enough credit in the bank to get kicked quite a few times before eventually they receive one kick too many and are pushed over the edge.

Learning organizations, however, are fun to work in and attract talent.

Why when some businesses just want to get the job done ... are others obsessed with fashion and fiction?

Why do some organizations talk tough about being profit-driven and focused on shareholder returns, but then run off and flirt with every passing idea that takes their fancy?

You know the sort of initiatives I mean: European Quality Awards, Investors in People, Total Quality Management and so on.

Don't get me wrong – there is nothing wrong with any of these ideas in their own right. The problems start in the way they are embraced.

Companies suffering stress approach these ideas in the same way that scouts go about collecting badges: they become an end in themselves, disconnected from the main thrust of the business, with more importance attached to the number of plaques in the reception than the impact on the organization.

The first step that some organizations took when embarking on Total Quality Management (TQM) initiatives was the appointment of a lost middle manager as TQM champion. At this point almost everyone else in the organization heaved a huge sigh of relief and thought:

> **'Thank God for that – at least I don't
> have to worry about quality any more.'**

Approached in this way, the only impact of these initiatives will be extra cost and a frantic flurry of last-minute action just before an audit is due, which will distract people from their day-to-day business but at least ensures they pass the audit!

This type of behaviour is utterly daft but it happens up and down the land in every type of organization, from family businesses through to giant PLCs and government departments.

It is interesting how many people I meet who say;

> **'I totally agree with you but not in my organization – we don't behave like that'**

And the sad thing is, they all really believe it!

But it doesn't change the facts. This stuff happens and it happens in companies where they repeatedly say it doesn't.

Why do some top teams work together ... whilst others pursue separate dreams?

I would never have believed how much animosity and rampant, mutual dislike exists in management teams charged with co-operating together for the good of an organization if I had not seen it with my own eyes.

No-one can choose their own family and you don't always get the opportunity to choose your colleagues, but when you accept a job within a team you have a responsibility to put personal animosity to one side for the good of the organization.

But does that happen? Does it hell!

In some organizations, personal vendettas are allowed to bubble to the surface non-stop and the amount of both personal effort and organizational resource that is wasted as a result can be frightening.

The issue with many of these managers is of course that the money they are wasting is not their own: it belongs to shareholders or comes as a grant from some government pot or other. If it were their own money then they might not behave in quite the same way, though I have to say that even in owner-run organizations I work with I have witnessed some pretty bizarre and wasteful behaviour.

> **But at least in owner-run organizations
> it is their own money they are wasting!**

Why do some organizations know exactly when to move before the need is even clear ... whilst others consistently hesitate to act?

An organization in tune with its workforce and customers not only senses problems and opportunities before they break, but also often has the cohesion and confidence to turn direction on a sixpence. For these organizations the ability to let things go is as important as the ability to pick things up.

In contrast I have known organizations caught like rabbits in car headlights, paralyzed by the fear of changing market conditions. In the end they would rather waste half a year on despair and acrimony than act boldly whilst they can still make a difference.

Prevarication and hesitation are without doubt the scourge of organizations.

Why do some companies thrive on constant challenge ... when others make even success seem hard work?

This becomes a lot clearer when you consider how people find jobs in the first place. For many people their whole career history is laced with luck and chance: being in the job market when a certain company was recruiting, seeing a certain advert, knowing someone who knew someone. Many people not in a true vocation have little real idea about the job or company they start working for before they actually start the job.

Some people pick losers and are repeatedly made redundant, or take several jobs before they find something that fits. Other people pick winners in the job lottery, walk into their first position and stay there all their working life. I know people in business that fell into the right job and have succeeded beyond their wildest dreams and even now cannot believe their own luck.

Nothing wrong with that from a personal point of view, but the last thing these people want to do is rock the boat by pushing themselves or indeed anyone else (except those lower down the pecking order) out of their comfort zones.

This inevitably creates stuffy, complacent business. What incentive is there for these people to take risks or leave when they don't think they will ever find another job half as cushy as the current one?

What is more, when an employee has several years of service under their belt, disgruntled employers will duck the issue, thinking that they will be too costly and difficult to move on.

How does stress impact on the performance of an organization?

Can a stressed organization still be successful, even if not as successful as it might otherwise be?

How widespread is the impact of stress? Does it spread far wider than just lost revenue?

My observations over the last few years have led me to believe that Corporate Stress is a fundamental problem for any organization that suffers from it. No matter who they are, Corporate Stress will impact on every aspect of how they perform.

One of the unfortunate characteristics of Corporate Stress is that it has a multiplier effect as it spreads out across an organization. Starting at the top it will accelerate away, breaking down any consistency and pulling different departments in different directions until eventually it sends the entire organization out of control. Every management level adds its own agenda crisis to the one above until there is so much confusion that confusion starts to become culturally acceptable.

Balance is lost and issues that should be easy to solve suddenly become much harder to deal with. Decision-making criteria are stretched out of shape, tasks that the organization has been handling well stop working and the whole 'health' of the organization starts to suffer.

Relationships break down both inside and outside the organization.

Loss of focus and concentration caused by stress has a dramatic effect on everyone. Personal and corporate confidence nosedive and a once satisfactorily performing organization will start to go off the rails. Both staff and organization enter a downward spiral with corporate performance damaging corporate morale, which further damages performance.

All the classic symptoms of stress in humans come to the surface: anxiety, too much to do in too little time and an inability to function properly.

What is interesting, however, is that Corporate Stress is rarely caused by too much good old-fashioned hard work but by a feeling of collective loss of control brought on by being pulled in different ways.

The ability of people to step up a gear in response to a genuine and focused need is phenomenal; consider the reaction of the general public to any national disaster for example. We are not generally shy of hard work if it is for the right cause; but when we sniff hypocrisy and what we interpret as incompetence, our will to contribute plummets.

What neither people nor organizations can withstand is contradiction and confusion; this is what causes Corporate Stress.

I have observed two distinctly different forms of Corporate Stress in organizations, both of which have different implications.

The first of these is acute Corporate Stress when organizations are in the grip of a near disaster and the second is chronic Corporate Stress. which is much more invidious and occurs when organizations have started to accept the unacceptable.

Acute Corporate Stress

Acute Corporate Stress is the most easily diagnosed. Something is clearly wrong and this will be evident in its financial performance. In the worst cases I have witnessed, a type of organizational schizophrenia takes hold, with conflicting decision-making criteria and behaviour very much in evidence.

I have seen small organizations run by two partners that hardly converse despite sitting within spitting distance of each other, both ordering the same people to do different things.

I have also observed giant PLCs and government departments where supposed colleagues direct whole divisions as if they were private armies in pursuit of incongruent goals.

The good news in these situations is that this type of crisis is hard to ignore, that there is little alternative to taking action and that there are several courses of action that are proven to help. We will look at these later in the book.

The bad news, of course, is that if action is not taken the organization is on a fast track to failure.

Chronic Corporate Stress

Chronic Corporate Stress is the real threat to organizations because it is far less easy to spot and deal with. It is caused either by the gradual erosion of the core purpose of an organization or a consistent and insidious degradation of personal and corporate behaviour and relationships.

Chronic Corporate Stress has now reached epidemic proportions in the West and is endemic within organizations of all sizes, costing shareholders and taxpayers billions in lost returns and wasted resources.

Chronic Corporate Stress is now so established in some organizations that it has got to the point where the resulting performance of the organization is considered to be normal.

As with all types of stress, it attacks the self-confidence of those that suffer from it. Few sufferers are initially able to recognize the scale of the impact it is having and fewer still are willing to stand up and admit it publicly.

Corporate Stress encourages organizations to accept ordinary as OK, hide their weaknesses and freeze out whistle blowers. The situation is often made worse by the fact that many organizations try to alleviate the symptoms through the use of various stress management techniques rather than actually addressing the root causes of the stress in the first place.

Every frustrating, bureaucratic, slow, self-obsessed organization you have ever dealt with will have been suffering Corporate Stress; but let's not forget that it is an illness like any other and should be treated as such, rather than as a cause for blame.

Another notable feature of Corporate Stress is that it is no respecter of ability and targets the most able as hard as everyone else. This becomes obvious when we see how fast successful organizations can experience a dramatic collapse in their fortunes.

> **Have you ever asked yourself why becoming a business case-study is so often the kiss of death?**

Why do so many companies featured in magazines and books as models of corporate excellence suddenly nosedive months later?

It is because the very things that created the companies' success often mutate into the seeds of their own downfall. Success today is never a guarantee of success tomorrow.

Corporate Stress in action:

Purpose and leadership are unclear
People can't make the best decisions
Action and communication lack focus
Time, money and opportunity are wasted
Morale, relationships and results suffer
Talent and value drain away

Without a clearly defined purpose it is impossible to have any clear leadership even from one individual. When leadership is expected from a whole team rather than just one person, the chances of delivering it become even less.

People are physically unable to make the right decisions as a result, because without clear leadership there are no agreed decision-making criteria on which to base decisions in the first place.

This is the most common situation I encounter when asked to help an organization. I am often asked to adjudicate on choices that even Solomon would be unable to judge. There is no right or wrong when there is no agreed goal, but that does not stop people trying.

I have on occasions had the misfortune to spend a whole day in a meeting listening to one person after another offer up views on the way forward. Each one is an equally valid route to achieving something; the problem is that no-one has agreed on the right 'something' to go for! Without an agreed goal these kinds of discussions cannot ever come to a satisfying conclusion!

It sounds crazy but it happens all the time and in local authorities, for example, it is the favoured method of operation. A desire to encourage democracy and foster a tolerant environment mutates into a debating society, where everyone has the right to speak but no-one takes responsibility to lead.

As a result, action and communication cannot fail but be confused and muddled. How can an organization remain focused when it has nothing clear to focus upon?

When an organization is insulated from the harsh realities of commercial necessity, as many organizations in the public sector are, it becomes completely viable for separate departments to pursue separate agendas. Indeed not only is it possible – it is hard to avoid.

And the situation will not be helped by several levels of management that exist in many large organizations. When people are not taking their lead from the horse's mouth but third or fourth hand, problems multiply. Chinese whispers can turn a comedy into a farce.

First-class internal communication is the exception, not the rule. Working with organizations for the first time I often discover that they are only devoting about 10–20% of the time, energy and resource required to communicate effectively internally.

Extending appropriate focus out to the market place is an even greater challenge that some organizations do not even start to embark upon, relying instead on an artificial façade.

In light of this it is impossible to avoid wasting time and money and missing opportunities. Not because anyone is behaving badly or maliciously, but because they are insufficiently prepared to avoid it. It is like sending under-prepared pilots with only eight hours' flying experience up to fight in the Battle of Britain: you must expect a frightening casualty rate.

That may have been unavoidable then, but it is never unavoidable now. It is simply poor practice.

No wonder morale, relationships and results suffer. Strong relationships require consistency and it is impossible for organizations to be consistent under these conditions. Who wants to work in an organization where the adequacy syndrome is so obviously manifest? It is impossible to be proud of an organization that is transparently suffering from low self-esteem and what is more, this crisis of corporate confidence is quickly going to transfer itself to individuals, resulting in a huge drop in performance. An ever-decreasing cycle of diminishing returns is inevitable.

Investor return takes a big hit and, most damagingly for the organization, its most talented and passionate employees will start to walk. Talent has a thousand homes but those with low self-esteem and convinced of their own weaknesses will be harder to move on than head lice at a primary school.

By the time that Corporate Stress is rife throughout an organization, the leadership team will be forced to take one of two routes:

- recognize and accept the existence of Corporate Stress, and respond rapidly and appropriately; or
- fail to respond to the challenge, allowing Corporate Stress to become institutional.

**Once Corporate Stress becomes institutional,
it becomes Corporate Denial.**

So how common is this, you might ask. Surely in a competitive environment this will weaken the organization to a point where it fails and is replaced?

This is partly true but not wholly so. Many organizations are in a situation where Corporate Denial can run and run before the company crumbles.

Examples are organizations that:

- are not competitively run but financed by grants;
- use fat stored up in the good years to keep going long after the problems have set in;
- are temporarily or permanently protected from competition;
- have competitors that are in the same state as they are – all equally bad, as with the utility companies of old;
- have relationships mandated by rules and regulations or protected by a lack of viable alternative;
- are incestuous, recruiting new directors and employees from other similar organizations so that no new blood comes in to blow the whistle on what is going on;
- are reviewed and measured by officials who have always worked under a similar culture and so accept the prevailing efficiency levels and style of leadership as totally normal; and
- have investors or regulators that are overstretched and, with bigger fish to fry, do not tend to worry about the 'small' problems.

The result is that Corporate Denial is commonplace: too many organizations have it too easy and too many organizations are insufficiently motivated to bother to sort problems out.

2.0

Companies in Denial

The importance of early diagnosis

wjm

The Corporate Denial effect

Figure 2.1 shows what happens when Corporate Denial takes hold: why a few degrees of lost focus result in potentially enormous losses in returns and efficiency.

On one axis, you have percentage of confusion and disagreement, and on the other, distance from decision-making.

Below the line we can see how strong leadership, agreed purpose, motivated staff and satisfied customers deliver maximum stakeholder value and amazing success.

Above the line we can see that distracted or divided leadership generates distrust and disillusionment amongst managers, wasted energy and low morale amongst employees, lost business, ultimately lost value to investors and finally weakened corporate relationships, and the institutional presence of Corporate Denial.

The percentages shown are not scientifically worked out but are meant to be indicative. They are based on my experience of talking to and working with many different organizations and the facts that those experiences have presented me with.

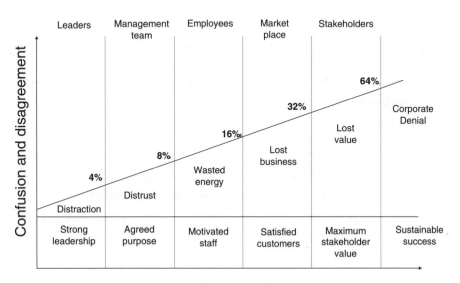

Fig 2.1   So what happens when Corporate Stress turns into Corporate Denial?

The figure of 60%-plus as an estimate of possible lost value experienced by organizations in Denial is not just my view but is based on candid opinions provided by finance directors I have spoken to of the value being lost in *their own* organizations as a result of untreated Corporate Denial. These gentlemen do not wish to be quoted!

With a 4% loss of focus equating to a colossal 64% reduction in productivity and stakeholder value, it is not hard to understand why Corporate Denial is the world's most damaging business taboo!

You might find these figures seem high, but bear in mind two things:

- in commercial situations, competitors may all be in the same boat and so all equally disadvantaged; and
- in public sector organizations, acceptable productivity is often based on the previous year – when Corporate Denial may already have been present – or benchmarked against similar organizations where, again, Corporate Denial may be established at an institutional level.

Corporate Denial can easily become so established that it is accepted as totally normal and quite simply the way things are done.

You only have to look at the EU to see the living personification of this. In environments such as these, appalling waste of every kind is accepted as a reasonable price for the maintenance of democracy.

But that still doesn't make it right and should not make it any more acceptable.

What are the symptoms of Corporate Denial?

I've already touched on some of these but if you think that your organization may be suffering stress or Corporate Denial, here is a simple checklist for you.

If you identify with more than a couple, it's time to start taking action!

To help, I have split the list in two. The first list contains general indicators of the presence of Corporate Denial; the second outlines the advanced symptoms.

Primary symptoms

Loss of purpose

This is one of the most obvious effects of Corporate Denial. If your organization is ploughing on regardless of an agreed direction, beware.

It is amazing how many organizations are unable to articulate what their core purpose is with any crispness and in a way that differentiates them from their competition. When you come across an organization that can, the difference is amazing.

Meaningless corporate values

The desire to go through a long-winded process to develop corporate values that are meaningless to everyone except those involved in their creation is a classic symptom.

Incredibly common in large PLCs, it is not only a waste of time but can actually be damaging. This type of badge engineering puts a gloss over deep-rooted problems and causes employees to become not only ineffective but also disenchanted.

Inability to focus

As common in large organizations as it is in small children, not only do some organizations lose their focus; they also actually lose the ability to focus.

Once the ability to focus is lost, there is no way back – short of a concerted campaign to address the root causes of Corporate Denial.

Management confusion

Often blamed on the quality of the management and addressed through re-cruitment or training, the problem is usually more fundamental.

If an organization's leadership or leadership communication is poor, management confusion will follow as surely as night follows day. No amount of new recruitment or management training can help an organization that is holed below the waterline. If the leadership is not up to scratch then new managers will struggle in exactly the same way as their predecessors did.

This is a case of removing the log from the leadership's eyes before attempting to remove the dust from the eyes of their bewildered and confused managers.

Muddled communication

It is only when an organization fails to communicate effectively with its market place that problems are sometimes noticed.

The first response to a drop in sales can be an immediate call for a new identity or a new advertising campaign. Rebranding may be expensive but it can be an easier pill to swallow than brutally honest self-examination of core relationships.

Less-than-scrupulously-honest communication companies will queue up to offload an organization's cash if they think there is money to be made; but putting a new face on a sick organization is purely papering over the cracks.

Muddled communication has often been the first point of contact for me with new clients. Together with my colleagues, David Birt and Tim Guy, we have worked with many organizations – from educational establishments through to small businesses and global PLCs – looking to communicate better.

When we have been able to convince a client of the need for clarity and consensus on their core purpose and the need to back up their market propositions with proven and demonstrable customer benefits, we have been able to achieve wonders. If we can get them to the stage where what they say to the market matches how they behave, then we are in business.

But convincing clients that the issues they face require more than cosmetic communication solutions and a quick logo change is sometimes a marathon task. The immediate reaction can be that you are stringing out the process for your own gain.

Many clients prefer easy, non-confrontational action that they can take immediately to challenging questions and the need to maybe think and behave in new ways.

Only when presented with unequivocal evidence are some clients prepared to take hard decisions, especially if it involves the agreement and support of peers or – worse still – bosses.

Trapped energy

As painful for organizations as it is for people, there is nothing more frustrating for a talented and committed manager than constantly being held back for no apparently good reason.

This is a fast-track way to waste revenue opportunities whilst losing your best talent at the same time.

Going back a few years, trapped energy was an almost universal problem in large organizations where waiting for a dead man's shoes was the only way forward. Now that people are faced with so many different career options, if you don't harness your talent quickly, it will be up and off.

Painful waste

For years now, the vast levels of waste prevalent in large organizations have been the saving grace of smaller companies trying to compete without the economies of scale of their larger cousins.

With the prevalence of concepts such as process re-engineering and just-in-time logistics management the traditional areas of waste are less common – but waste is still causing problems because of Corporate Denial.

However much you improve an organization's efficiency, if it is intent on doing the wrong things you will only help it do the wrong things better, faster and cheaper!

The rapid churn of managers from one post to another means that for every ten new initiatives started, only two or three ever reach fruition before the management move on and a fresh approach is tried.

Damaged morale

Morale is one of the intangible assets of an organization most at threat from and most undermined by modern management ideas.

Everything from contract working and home working through to hot desking are designed to reduce fixed costs. That's fine, but we must recognize the invisible cost of these modern management initiatives.

Despite the significant lifestyle benefits that many of these new ideas deliver to employees, each one severs another thread in the bond between employee and employer. This vital relationship is in danger of slipping further and further towards a simple financial transaction of money for labour.

If in addition to the trend for increased remoteness employees perceive the leadership team to be in any way avaricious, mercenary or plain lost, any interest that they may have in providing additional added value in terms of care for the future of the organization and its customers goes out of the window.

And with it goes their willingness to point out potential pitfalls or opportunities. They may well consider, in line with their mobile status, that it is easier to abandon ship and jump flea-like to another passing organization.

Corporate Denial claims another victim.

Inaction

I have seen inaction that you would not believe possible, such as major companies prepared to do nothing because of current or pending internal reorganizations.

It is enough to make you scream!

And with organizations reorganizing more often all the time, I can only see the situation getting worse.

Low corporate libido

Have you seen an organization with its head down and all its bounce gone?

It is as sad as it gets in organizational terms.

You know what is going on the second you walk into the office. Everybody looks that bit scruffier than they have a right to look. Even the office looks tired; there will be a notice board near the coffee machine with an advert for a 12-year-old Nissan next to a large sign saying, 'No unauthorized notices to be stuck on this board by order of H. Brown, Head of Personnel'.

People walk more slowly than they need to and the hourly trip to the toilet is eagerly anticipated. The most active sign of life is always outside the fire exit where furtive smokers gather, regardless of the rain, to predict who will be next to leave.

Customer service descends to an all-time low and the only people recruiting will be the complaints department.

Everything is a problem under these conditions and cost cutting is more important than growth, regardless of the idea; those with initiative are considered to be actually rather annoying.

This is the day-to-day reality for thousands of employees working in organizations suffering Corporate Denial.

Damaged relationships

It is hard for anyone to feel valued by a company in Denial. The inconsistency and indeed outright contradiction that is so common in organizations in Denial strangles relationships.

People have long memories and are usually willing and able to spread bad news fast. Organizations in Denial soon acquire a worse reputation than the office Romeo.

Trying to maintain a good relationship with an organization in Denial is like living with any type of addict; it's highly unpredictable and personally draining!

Advanced symptoms

If you recognize items on this list; it's time to be afraid – very afraid!

Management reshuffles

A killer sign! If you are reorganizing more than once every 18 months, the chances are you are suffering severe Corporate Denial.

In very rare cases, there may sometimes be a genuine need for this. But these will be few and far between, because the disruption that reorganization brings is too great for any sane organization to live with.

And the worst part is that it will be the same tired old faces who screwed up the last organization that get another chance to do it all again, while someone else picks up the mess they left behind. When everyone moves one job to the left, no-one can be blamed for anything.

Obsessions

When all else is moribund or collapsing around you, it is the perfect time to obsess. Nothing distracts from appalling ordinariness like an obsession.

The range of obsessions for companies in denial is almost endless; there is always something to obsess about that is more important than the organizations real weaknesses. For example:

- your personal job security;
- corporate confidentiality;
- devious customers;
- government policy changes;
- avoiding risks;
- company car policy;
- uniforms for security guards;
- water fountains; and
- parking spaces.

What obsessions do you recognize?

Introspection
Not far behind obsession in the Denial hall of fame comes introspection.

If all else fails, look inward for a solution.

Paranoia
Yes, they probably are out to get you; but when an organization is in Denial, everything seems to be a threat except of course the causes of Denial itself!

Those with much to hide are usually the most fearful of others and believe that everyone else operates under the same values as they do, which is true of paranoid organizations.

There is a well known saying that goes along the lines of:

Keep your friends close and your enemies closer still.

Organizations in Denial believe the reverse:

Keep everyone far away and your friends furthest of all.

Delusions
The brother of introspection, obsession and paranoia is delusion. The ability to believe exactly what you want to believe to be true (even though you are mile off!) is the last refuge of those in Denial.

And this does not have to be a temporary phenomenon either: those in the deep throws of Denial can make delusion last a lifetime.

Paralysis

Two years in the life of an organization suffering Corporate Denial.

1 Point zero minus six months: growing anticipation of the new organization is rife; most senior managers are preoccupied with networking amongst the organization's rising stars in order to be well positioned for advancement.

2 Point zero minus three months: the new organization is due shortly, so no-one will do anything in case it is seen to be wrong in light of the new structure.

3 Point zero minus one month: all senior managers desperately plead for a new job so the sins of last year's time-wasting can be hoofed off onto another poor unsuspecting victim.

4 Point zero: the planned reorganization is put back two months to accommodate the wishes of an intransigent director who keeps digging in his heels and refuses to be shunted into the tempting VP Internal Affairs job.

5 Point zero plus two months: another delay due to the CEO going on a world tour, followed by that well-deserved holiday.

6 Point zero plus four months: European integration plans emanating from the holding company puts all plans on hold.

7 Point zero plus ten months: at long last, management consultants recommend the existing plan goes ahead pending a fuller review of European integration.

8 Point zero plus twelve months: the original plan set to be announced.

9 Point zero plus twelve and a half months: hostile bid received; all bets off!

10 Point zero plus eighteen months: senior managers look forward to extremely generous takeover conditions and contemplating retirement.

… Recognize any of this, anyone?

Monopolistic behaviour

All monopolistic behaviour, whatever the justification, will lead to Corporate Denial.

Whatever business we are in, competition is an essential ingredient to long-term organizational health. Without competition, it is as impossible for an organization to become amazingly successful as it is for a lion to see a zebra as anything else but food.

Split personality
The split personality is the norm for organizations in Denial because there is in fact nothing holding it together apart from the financial shared interest of departments and directors.

Many organizations in Denial have got to the point where a split personality is considered totally normal and doesn't even justify a raised eyebrow. The idea of a business with integrity presenting a common front to investors, management, employees, customers and society is often openly scoffed at as a preposterous idea.

Relationship starvation
When things get really bad, organizations begin to feel the awful effects of re-lationship starvation. Open hostility between organizations that have to work together is a key sign of Denial, similar to the situation between countries when ambassadors are withdrawn. Hostility represents a complete breakdown of normal relations and must be confronted immediately as it can only lead to further damage. Relationship starvation kills companies.

Rigor mortis
OK, so this is a bit of an exaggeration – but it can feel like rigor mortis working in certain organizations!

How does Corporate Denial take hold?

Corporate Denial is, above all, an expert in disguise. It furnishes those affected with every possible reason not to recognize its existence. It doesn't come storm-ing through the front door announcing its arrival.

Similar to any type of addiction – be it drugs, alcohol or anything else – it can lead to some very devious behaviour, with those caught in its grasp desperate not to be found out.

It is also important to remember that it does not arrive overnight. The seed of Corporate Denial (Corporate Stress) can have a very long incubation period, during which the symptoms are far from obvious but the condition highly transferable.

And we must not forget the predilection of organizations suffering from Corporate Denial to play musical chairs. If at the first sign of problems you move everyone around from one job to the next, it is only going to make things worse.

Companies in Denial are good at making things worse for themselves: take the type of reward schemes that they operate, for example. Many of these schemes – rather than encouraging managers to push themselves harder and try out new ideas – actually work against innovation, with managers rewarded for avoiding mistakes and not upsetting anyone.

What started as a drive to remove old-fashioned management bullying often becomes an excuse for weak, disinterested management: the 'yes sir, no sir' faction being better looked after than those who rock the boat and make a few waves in an effort to drive change.

Another major contributor to the spread of Denial is the way organizations benchmark their performance. For many, this is a process of being better than competitors rather than being the best an organization can be.

Once we are happy to benchmark our success against other organizations suffering equally from Corporate Denial, we are in trouble, and moving rapidly to a market situation determined by the lowest common denominator.

This is a reverse SAS-type mentality:

Who's worst loses!

But we mustn't overlook the fact that it is often as hard for those at the centre of Corporate Denial as it is for those who suffer the fallout.

Many of those at the centre of an organization and charged with responsibility for leading it eventually become aware of the condition, but feel unable to deal with it.

They are likely to believe that there is a personal stigma attached to Corporate Denial and will be very unwilling to admit its presence. Corporate Denial robs both the organization as a whole and its individuals of self-esteem.

Some key directors will believe that the organization's problems are entirely their own fault and will close in upon themselves. This isn't helpful, however, as it makes them even more reluctant to take risks or highlight the situation to others as they believe any action will only accelerate their personal unmasking as a fraud and subsequent downfall.

> **There is nothing else in organizational terms quite like the loneliness of the Corporate Denial sufferer.**

Corporate ghettos

When the personality of an organization breaks up, individuals develop their own cult following. One organization I worked with could be compared to the House of Commons: there was a Prime Minister and a Leader of the Opposition, a small and ineffectual cabinet, a swarm of marginalized back benchers, and a disgruntled civil service picking up the pieces.

Not the best way to run a company, but not that uncommon either. The number of small businesses I have worked with where there are two key principals who no longer have any meaningful communication (although they may actually sit opposite each other) is frightening.

A reaction common to many organizations in Denial is the establishment of corporate ghettos, where individuals gather together in the absence of proper leadership to form informal but fiercely defensive groups.

These separate ghettos become the mainstay of internal communication and loyalty switches from the organization to the ghetto. All socialising and as much working contact as possible is restricted to other members of the ghetto.

Ghettos can have amazing influence on the lives of all concerned and in time come to dominate the entire culture and effectiveness of an organization.

Passive Corporate Denial: the innocent victims

But the cost of Denial is felt far wider than the borders of the organization itself. In addition to employees who suffer, so do investors and customers.

Welcome to passive Corporate Denial. The innocent victims are:

- investors, who lose out on the chance to co-operate and input ideas into the organization – they also lose out financially because it is their money that is lost and wasted;
- employees, who lose out in terms of satisfaction and development; and
- customers, who lose out in terms of choice, value and enjoyment.

Customer service? You must be joking!

Corporate Denial and our support systems

But the problems do not stop there.

To add insult to injury, it is unfortunate that the very places we look to for help in dealing with Denial are hotbeds of Denial themselves.

Government, professional services firms, consultancies and academia are all exactly the environments where Corporate Denial is most at home.

How can an organization help us if at its very core it is suffering the same problems?

What we tend to get are solutions aimed at symptoms rather than causes – which in the long run allows Corporate Denial more time to become further established – and not the help we desperately need to confront and deal with our own Denial.

Many professional service firms are notoriously bad at getting beyond personal networking to establish good relationships with all contacts. This holds them back commercially and also limits their ability to add value to their clients.

Relationships are generally foreign ground to professional service firms. Relationships are far too 'touchy-feely' for consultants and so have for a long time been played down in importance with regard to organizational growth.

In many of these organizations, dress down Friday is seen as risky and getting seriously drunk is the only permissible excuse for showing any type of emotion.

Most of these firms are more comfortable dealing in matters of fact and intellect than they are in emotions, so they are unlikely to encourage their clients to think about corporate relationships and the associated issues of displaying and managing corporate emotion.

Some indeed might go further and argue that a number of professional service firms are in fact emotionally crippled and therefore completely unable to advise in the area of organizational relationships.

Corporate Denial in perspective

When one starts to consider Corporate Denial on a global basis, the scale of the problem becomes quite daunting.

- What percentage of global GDP is being lost?
- How many billions of dollars do investors lose a year?

- What is the cost in personal terms to employees and customers?
- How much does Corporate Denial slow down the rate of global progress?

If Corporate Denial is a universal cause for concern there are strong reasons to believe that some regions are more threatened than others and that the historic success of Western countries puts them at greatest threat.

The plutocratic American economy, preoccupied with legal and financial solutions, is always potentially at risk. Prone to introspection and an attitude that regards anything non-American with deep suspicion, the US must be vulnerable to Denial.

The saving grace for the US, however, is a culture firmly rooted in customers.

The European preference for bureaucracy is also a reason for concern. The EU itself is so deep in Denial it is hard to be optimistic for its future. Hope for Europe must rest on a long tradition of innovation and invention, and the belief that commercial interests will override political infighting.

The picture for the Asia Pacific region looks healthier. From Japan through China to India, there has long been a strong work ethic and a belief system based around the family, personal honour and the importance of sacrifice for the greater good. Hospitality, the value placed on relationships and the accepted importance of mutual respect will help these regions prevent the spread of Corporate Denial and increase their competitiveness against the West.

Corporate Denial is never black and white and it is not as simple as saying one region will prosper against another because we all have free will and the ability to either fight back or give in.

What is without doubt, however, is that the West has a fight on its hands and widespread Corporate Denial can only hold it back.

Beating Corporate Denial

Corporate Denial is slow-burn to start with but, as we've seen, can eventually be whipped up into a firestorm.

Early diagnosis is vital: it is impossible to recognize and respond to the symptoms too early, and you don't have to be a CEO or managing director either.

Anyone of any influence who has the determination and guts can start the fight back. It doesn't matter whether we are managers, non-executives, investors, employees or a member of the leadership team itself; we all have the responsibility as well as the opportunity to act.

Why does it matter?

It matters for every reason I have already described. But what makes Corporate Denial the world's most damaging business taboo is not only the billions of dollars a year lost globally, but the fact that failure to confront Denial damages each and every one of us personally.

At its heart, Corporate Denial destroys organizational effectiveness and relationships; so to confront Denial, we must understand what makes organizations effective in the first place.

3.0 Understanding Effectiveness

What makes organizations tick?

wjm

Seeking the source of human effectiveness

I am convinced that there isn't a quick fix solution in the world that can solve the problems of Corporate Denial. One quick fix after another is after all what has contributed to the situation in the first place.

To make progress we must go back to basics. There is no way any of us can lead amazingly successful organizations until we have a clear idea about the basic principles of human effectiveness.

And how better to understand basic human effectiveness than by referring back to Stephen R. Covey's book – *The Seven Habits of Highly Effective People*?

With over ten million copies sold worldwide, this book has become the standard text for people wishing to improve their personal effectiveness and achieve greater levels of personal happiness.

Stephen Covey examines the way we look at the world and the impact that has on the way we think and behave. He investigates how our core beliefs influence our everyday effectiveness and the likelihood of our achieving our life's goals.

At the start of his book, he describes the way we look at the world as a *social paradigm*. To quote Stephen, he describes a social paradigm as:

> *'the way we see the world – not in terms of our visual sense of sight, but in terms of perceiving, understanding, interpreting ... [and] the source of our attitudes and behaviours. We cannot act with integrity outside of them.'*

My understanding of a social paradigm is that it is a lens through which we see life; it determines the way we see/interpret everything that comes into our life. It determines our image of ourselves, our view of others and of our surroundings; in fact, it shapes our relationships with everything we encounter.

Our social paradigm isn't static and evolves naturally as we experience different things. We can, if we wish, change our social paradigm through education or training and exposing ourselves to new ideas.

Whatever social paradigm we use defines reality as we see it; yet despite this, most of us consider ourselves to be totally objective. What we think of as objective is of course in reality subjective, as the paradigm that we view life through will actually have already shaped our vision of reality.

Our experiences train each of us to individually view the same issue differently, which is why people look at the same facts and then draw different but potentially equally valid conclusions.

This also means that, as our social paradigm evolves through exposure to new experiences, our view of reality will change with it.

Connecting social paradigms to our personality

If social paradigms are crucial to our development, growth and prosperity, how do they fit with concepts that we are more familiar with such as our personality and character?

- Social paradigm: a set of principles for interpreting and judging how people should act, and interact.
- Character: the basic qualities and values that determine an individual's behaviour and attitudes.
- Personality: the expression of an individual's character and principles through their behaviour, attitudes, emotional responses, relationships and interests.

Which together means that the social paradigm we inherit or adopt as we grow up is our model for interpreting and judging how people should act and interact. It conditions our basic character, which in turn determines our behaviour, attitudes, emotional responses, relationships and interests, which we express through our personality.

What is the most effective social paradigm?

Having looked at the mechanics of social paradigms and how they shape our character and personality, Stephen Covey goes further.

From his own experience, and with reference to many of the books written on the subject of personal effectiveness over the last 200 years, he identified two specific social paradigms associated with achieving personal effectiveness.

He highlighted two key social paradigms: the *Character Ethic* and the *Personality Ethic*.

The Character Ethic

The Character Ethic as described by Stephen Covey is based on 150 years of writing about personal effectiveness from about 1770 to 1920. Those that adhere to the Character Ethic believe in the fundamental idea that there are principles or natural laws that govern human effectiveness.

Stephen describes these as:

> *'natural laws in the human dimension that are just as real, just as unchanging and unarguably there as laws such as gravity are in the physical dimension.'*

They are in fact the fundamental principles behind human morality and nearly all the world's great religions, and have been the basis of most of the great civilizations in history – certainly those that managed to achieve any significant harmony and stability.

The Character Ethic is based on the fact that true personal effectiveness and enduring happiness can *only ever* be achieved when a person integrates these principles into their basic character.

The Personality Ethic

The second social paradigm that Stephen Covey identifies was the Personality Ethic. He noticed a marked change in literature from around 1920 that focused on enhancing personal effectiveness. He recognized that the vast bulk of literature from the 1920s onwards was focused on varying aspects of personal improvement.

If the Character Ethic is principle-based and concentrates on who you are, the Personality Ethic is practice-based and concentrates on what you do.

The Personality Ethic sees personal effectiveness as a function of personality and public image. It concentrates on skills and techniques and uses power-base strategies to dominate others, alternating between coercion, intimidation, manipulation and influence to get what is required.

It teaches that you can copy the behaviours of effectiveness by observing what effective people do without having to understand and adopt their beliefs. It suggests that you can mask underlying character traits by learning and mimicking the effective behaviour, 'good manners' and etiquette of highly effective people.

With positive mental attitude replacing fundamental beliefs, the heart of the Personality Ethic is the 'get rich quick', short-cut approach that promises fast results to everyone.

The secret of personal effectiveness

Stephen Covey is unequivocal in his view that the Personality Ethic is a fraud. He believes that its predominance in literature providing guidance on how to become successful during the latter part of the 20th century was a major retrograde step for Western society and that much unhappiness and frustration has been caused as a result.

The road to becoming highly effective, then, is a straight and narrow one.

Only if we adhere fully to the principles outlined within the Character Ethic can we become highly effective and succeed in the pursuit of appropriate goals.

So are organizations very different?

Why don't highly effective people always run successful organizations? And why aren't all successful organizations run by highly effective people?

We have all seen successful organizations being run by people who don't come close to being highly effective, whilst people we know to be highly effective sometimes work in unremarkable, underperforming companies that demonstrate every symptom of Corporate Denial.

What is going on then?

The answer lies not in re-examining the laws that govern personal effectiveness but in reviewing the similarities and intrinsic differences between highly effective people and organizations.

So where do we start?

We know that highly effective people:

- control all decision-making from one place – their brain;
- coordinate thought and action centrally in their brain and can make their mouth, hands, feet and everything in between do what they want when they want (well, almost everything!);
- have a single mouthpiece; and
- are driven by a single social paradigm – the Character Ethic.

Organizations, on the other hand:

- have multiple decision-making points and use multiple decision-making criteria;
- cannot centrally control every aspect of their operation;
- struggle to send uncorrupted messages from the centre outwards and are often unable to receive incoming messages from distant parts of the organization at all;
- are driven by a variety of conflicting influences;
- may try and influence behaviour through corporate values without defining and weighting underlying motivations, failing to make them either relevant or meaningful to anyone apart from the team that created them;
- are unlikely to be able to manage relationships in a consistent manner without making a determined effort to do so; and
- may have a leadership team covertly hostile to each other's motivations, beliefs, individual social paradigms and ideas about corporate culture.

All of which makes it easy to understand why the majority of organizations struggle to maximize their potential!

Table 3.1

Individuals	Organizations
Social paradigm	Working culture
Character	Corporate values
Personality	Corporate identity

A working model of organizational effectiveness

Based on these differences, it is clear that the model that explains human behaviour will require a degree of adaptation if we want to make it appropriate to organizations.

We can use a similar format to the original model but with some key differences (see Table 3.1).

Whereas the individual model defines the links between social paradigm, human character and our personality, the new organizational model defines the connections between an organization's working culture, corporate values and, ultimately, corporate identity.

Let's look at each of these in more detail.

Working culture

A working culture is the way an organization shapes its values, identity, behaviour and relationships, in the same way that a social paradigm conditions the character, personality, behaviour and attitudes of an individual.

It determines the way an organization interprets everything it sees and touches; the organization's self-image and branding, and its attitude to its employees, customers, partners, competitors and the society and environment in which it operates.

How does it work and how does it compare with a social paradigm?

- Working culture works in a similar way to social paradigms but involves the control of multiple inputs and multiple outputs.
- It is applicable only in the context of the organization's specific purpose.
- It controls the conduct of the organization as a whole and any individual personally representing the organization.

In an ideal world, every organization would operate a single working culture in the same way as a person is driven by one social paradigm.

But as organizations have no inbuilt natural mechanism for creating a single working culture, it becomes a prime responsibility of any designated leader who wants to lead a unified organization to create one.

There are as many different ways to create a unified working culture as there are leaders. But if a leadership team fails to fulfil its responsibilities for creating a single working culture, the result will be a split culture.

Split or multiple working cultures dramatically affect an organization's focus, damage its effectiveness and limit its ability to maintain consistent relationships, producing the perfect breeding ground for Corporate Denial.

Balancing the use of working culture and individual social paradigms

Individuals working within an organization fulfil two roles, firstly as a representative of the organization and secondly as themselves. This means that they must balance the use of the organization's working culture for representing the organization with their own social paradigm when representing themselves.

Whatever the prescribed working culture; individuals are always free to conduct personal relationships under their own social paradigm.

This means that working cultures apply to:

- all organizational relationships;
- all organizational decision-making;
- creating and implementing corporate strategy;
- day-to-day operations;
- performance reviews;
- personal reviews; and
- all customer contact.

Social paradigms apply to personal relationships.

Any personal relationship will be governed by normal social paradigms. Highly effective people will apply the Character Ethic and less effective people will use whatever social paradigm they are conditioned by.

This is why people applying an organization's working culture to make really tough, hard-nosed business decisions one minute may still conduct their own personal networking using their own social paradigm that may be different from the working culture in force in the organization at the time.

Balancing a prevailing working culture with our own social paradigm can sometimes be difficult. We may be tempted to:

- subjugate our true personality in order to fit in with the working culture of the organization we work for; or
- take advantage of the unreality and impermanence of our working existence to do things that we couldn't afford to do or wouldn't dream of doing as an individual governed by our own social paradigm.

If things get to a point where a leader of an organization is for any reason unable to create a single working culture or feels that the working culture agreed by the organization conflicts with their own social paradigm, they must consider their future carefully if they want to protect their dignity and integrity.

Corporate values

Corporate values are the expression of an organization's working culture.

Trying to develop corporate values for an organization without understanding the underlying working culture is like going down to the motor show and spending two days in detailed discussions with the sales staff on the Rolls-Royce and Ferrari stands, but without any idea whether or not you can actually afford to buy and run one!

It is utterly pointless – not that it has ever stopped thousands of ultimately disappointed companies from trying to do it.

For corporate values to work effectively, they must be built on one amalgamated working culture rather than weakly collecting ideas together from several different cultures prevailing across an organization.

When different ideas are merely collected together it is usually quite transparent that the chosen values fail to impress or satisfy anyone.

Corporate identity

Corporate identity is the organizational equivalent of human personality. Corporate values should determine corporate identity in the way that character determines personality.

Any identity not built on carefully formulated and culturally relevant values is, to paraphrase Prince Charles, a carbuncle on the face of corporate life. It is a disgrace without excuse.

To make matters worse, the general perception of corporate identity is still invariably limited to the visual aspects of an organization's public expression, such as branding and logos.

Corporate identity is in fact much more than this: it is the complete expression of an organization's working culture and values, including employee behaviour, corporate policy, relationships, communication, advertising, buildings and signage, as well as visual branding and logos. The last two elements are only the final expression of corporate identity – the icing on the cake, if you like – and not its sole meaning.

When British Telecom rebranded to BT, I had one hell of a job generating excitement about the impact that the new brand was going to have on the 2500 sales and service staff that were talking to major clients.

If you wanted to talk about painting lorries, new staff uniforms or putting a new logo on top of the BT Tower, no problem. Ensuring that the changes in the organization were reflected in the behaviour of the 2500 people representing BT to its most important customers, however, was hardly on the agenda.

This is a mistake being repeated regularly by organizations both large and small, and reflects the business world's fixation with cosmetic solutions.

> **Logos are sexy, culture change is hard graft.**

The larger the organization, the greater the problem this becomes, to the point that insufficiently holistic or rigorous approaches to corporate identity are putting large organizations at risk of systematically failing to deliver a consistent face to customers.

4.0 Inside Success

The theory of relative performance

wjm

The spectrum of success

Does success mean the same to every organization?

Are all working cultures equal or are some more equal than others?

Is it time for organizations to start making life choices, as people do?

To answer these questions we need to understand exactly what success means to different organizations and what effect an organization's situation has on its attitude to success.

This is where my 'theory of relative performance' comes into play.

Although it contains a couple of diagrams, this is more about the spirit of theory than the exact science of it. It is not meant to baffle but simply illustrate some key facts of organizational life.

The theory is built around two principles:

- required organizational performance (ROP) – designed to help to illustrate the level of performance that an organization will be required to deliver in order to successfully achieve its stated goals, in any given market, at any given time; and
- actual organizational performance (AOP) – designed to help to illustrate how effective and tightly focused an organization must be to ensure that it closely matches the performance required to achieve stated goals, with the minimum of waste and unnecessary effort.

Required organizational performance (ROP)

ROP demonstrates that the same levels of performance will produce markedly different levels of success for different organizations in different situations; and, in return, that the same degree of success can be achieved by different organizations putting in different levels of performance.

ROP is based on the interplay between two key variables and suggests that by linking these two variables we can predict the level of performance that an organization must deliver to succeed.

- Duration of competition, defined as the period of time that an organization is *actively planning for*, that is to say the time they are willing to wait until the benefits of their decisions start to materialize. Every decision that we make comes with an attached timescale – are we willing and can we afford to invest three years in a project, or do we want results within the next three months or even the next three days?
- Degree of competition, which reflects the openness of the market place to new entrants and how fiercely other organizations are competing for the same customers. The degree of competition is determined by market conditions.

A number of issues impact on both variables.

Variable one – how long is the organization planning to compete for?

Is the organization happy with short term success?

Many businesses have no long-term aspirations; they quite simply want to achieve something and then move on. This applies at times to both task-orientated commercial and non-commercial organizations.

Do those running the organization have any interest in building long-term relationships and long-term success?

Many individuals tasked with running an organization have little or no personal interest in the long-term future of it and limit their interest to the time that they will be responsible for (and indeed benefit from) the organization's success. This can happen regardless of the aspirations of the organization's stakeholders.

Is it even possible to contemplate a long-term future or is the future too uncertain?

Some markets are so changeable that any detailed investment and planning for the future proves largely futile.

Would a long-term view damage short-term success?

There are times when too great a concern for the future will detract attention from short-term priorities and damage an organization's current prospects, which will in turn damage long-term prospects as well.

What is the prevailing business culture in the region?

The demands of the stock markets in Europe and America may put different pressures on an organization from those of, say, a Japanese competitor.

A Japanese organization may benefit from a longer-term view of success. With returns expected more slowly, a stronger foundation of trust can be built between the organization, its shareholders and the market place.

Variable two – how competitive is the market?

Is it regulated or controlled?

To what degree is free competition restricted? The greater the restrictions, the more freedom organizations are given to behave how they want.

Is the market commercial or non-commercial?

Non-commercial markets do not attract the same degree of interest as competitive ones, changing the nature of the pressure on non-commercial organizations to continually perform to their very best.

Are there geographic barriers to entry?

If a service can only be provided by a local supplier, then the lack of a viable alternative may remove the pressure on an organization, at least for a period of time.

Can a short-term monopoly be set up?

There may be a number of reasons why an organization can exploit a short-term monopoly, such as the level of required investment, for example.

Can legal barriers to entry be erected?

If an organization can find legal ways to hinder the entry of other firms into a market, such as the use of controlling patents etc, then it can prove invaluable.

How fast is the market changing?

A rapidly moving market can work in two ways. Entry of newcomers will be prevented if change is so fast that they cannot recoup their investment. On the other hand, rapidly changing markets can erase the benefits of being an established player – encouraging new entrants to the market.

When we relate the degree of market competition to planned duration of competition, we can work out the ROP an organization needs to succeed!

With duration of competition on one axis and degree of competition on the other, we can plot the ROP for success.

ROP runs diagonally across Figure 4.1 from bottom left to top right, with poor performance at zero and high performance at ten.

What is this telling us?

- It starts to demonstrate the difference between people and organizations.
- It starts to answer the questions as to why so many poorly run organizations survive and even grow.
- It starts to explain why Corporate Denial is so widespread.

Looking at this diagram, we can see what most of us have long known but have somehow been persuaded is not true – that bad organizations can do OK.

That success is not all equal and that there is only an indirect relationship between performance and success.

On a surface level, this appears to run in the face of Stephen Covey's views about effectiveness and his adherence to the belief that the only way to become successful was through applying the morally correct Character Ethic.

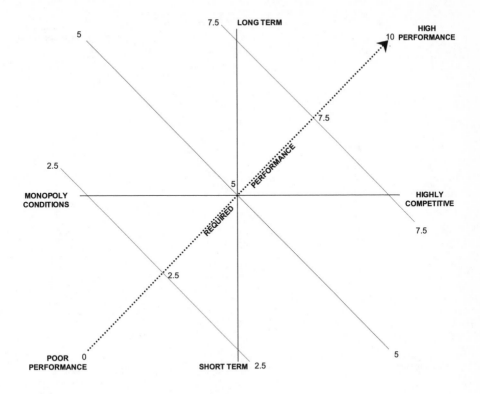

Fig. 4.1 ROP

But on reflection maybe it does not. Stephen always views success as a long-term issue and I think he is right. What we are looking at here is not success in his sense of the word but it is success in the sense of, 'What can I get away with and still make money?'

And the more time you spend around organizations, the more you realize that there are plenty of people and plenty of organizations for whom that is just fine.

To understand exactly how ROP works we can plot several different organizational scenarios, as shown in Figure 4.2, and see what the implications are for each situation.

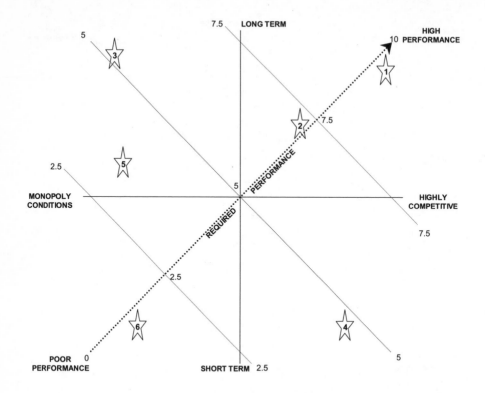

Fig. 4.2 ROP applied

Let's examine these one by one.

1   **Highly competitive and a long-term view.** An organization in a highly
    competitive market place and committed to enduring success has no
    choice but to perform to the maximum. This is a tough situation: only
    ten out of ten for performance delivered by a tightly knit effective team is
    going to work. *Success under these conditions is amazing success!*

2   **Reasonably competitive and a medium-term outlook.** Despite delivering
    a weaker performance than organization 1, this organization still achieves
    its goals. Performance is good enough to bring success but what could it
    achieve if it raised its performance? *This is the fate of far too many reasonably
    successful owner-run businesses.*

3   **Little competition but long-term goals.** Now we are getting into civil
    service territory. With little or no direct competition but the desire to
    deliver value for a period of time, there are likely to be far too many
    independent behaviours and personal agendas getting in the way of

improving relationships and performance. Performance can slip right down to halfway without significant sanctions, which is probably a fair reflection of the behaviour and relationships of some long-established institutions. This is also the ground that used to be occupied by public utilities and it is little surprise that service was so consistently dire. With no competition and little if any plans to change the world, even the incompetent were able to flourish, as we have often witnessed. *School report – must try harder!*

4   **Significant competition but short-term window of opportunity.** Typical of your average ticket tout, these guys will probably only meet each customer once and are relying on a constant supply of new buyers. No relationships are needed with customers. There is however a real need to be highly efficient and maintain a careful balance of supply and demand, so supply relationships and a canny mind are critical. *No requirement for fancy customer service.*

5   **Monopoly conditions and few long-term aspirations.** This is typical of some local service providers such as plumbers, electricians and heating engineers. There is so much demand and so few handy men that all they need to do is buy an old van, put an advert in *Yellow Pages* and turn on the mobile phone. *Money for old rope.*

6   **Near monopoly and extreme short-termism.** This is exploitation mode. When an organization has something that is in great demand and in limited supply, it is pretty much free to behave as it wishes. This is typical of the environment before the internet bubble burst, with investors clambering all over each other to throw money at internet companies. Organizations can make a lot of money very quickly this way at the expense of the needy, the gullible and the greedy. *Take the money and run!*

Why is this helpful?

What does this mean to those running organizations?

Firstly, being able to think about how well an organization needs to perform to succeed can help us plan overall resource levels more accurately and help us determine how hard we must work to get things right.

Secondly, getting *'everything'* right is very:

- expensive
- time-consuming
- distracting
- difficult.

This means that:

- too much effort and we fail because we are too slow, too expensive and take our eyes off the market for too long, trying to get everything too perfect; and
- too little effort and we fail through not keeping our customers happy.

An organization needs to balance every aspect of its performance in order to perform to its best. A company is only as good as its weakest link and therefore throwing time and investment at one area without considering others is pure folly. There is no point using a beautiful box to deliver a cheap and nasty present – you will soon be found out!

Actual organizational performance (AOP)

Gaining a greater understanding of the ROP for success is useful, but it is when we combine this understanding with a knowledge of what drives the AOP that we can really start to apply our new-found knowledge effectively.

And just as there are two variables needed to define ROP, so there are also two variables in determining AOP.

AOP is determined by:

- relationship effectiveness – the correlation between an organization's working culture and the proven, morally correct, natural laws of relationship effectiveness, as described earlier; and
- degree of focus – how efficiently the organization is focused on its working culture.

Placing the effectiveness of an organization's working culture on one axis and degree of focus on the other, we can illustrate AOP.

AOP runs diagonally across Figure 4.3 from bottom left to top right, with poor performance at zero and with high performance at ten.

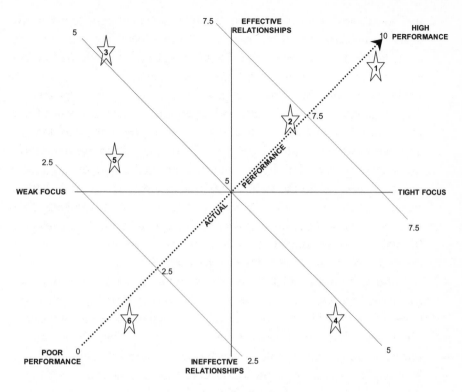

Fig. 4.3 AOP

To understand how AOP works, we can use the same 'organizational scenarios' that we used to illustrate ROP and look at the implications on effectiveness and focus.

1   **Highly competitive and a long-term view.** (*Success under these conditions is amazing success!*) Nothing less than a highly effective working culture will cut the mustard for this organization. There can be no cutting relationship corners here: employees, customers, investors and even the leadership team must be treated with the respect they are due. Only a tightly focused organization building the right working culture will deliver the right result. This organization must go to some lengths to ensure that its chosen working culture is fully bought into by everyone involved. *If they get it all right the sky is the limit.*

2   **Reasonably competitive and a medium-term outlook.** (*The fate of far too many reasonably successful owner-run businesses.*) This organization also has to be quite good; it must develop a reasonably effective working culture

and work hard to ensure that the whole organization goes pretty much in the same direction. A bit more effort on its focus and relationships could take it into another league. *Considerable ability, but currently lacks the ambition and endeavour to make it to the Premier League.*

3   **Little competition but long-term goals.** (*School report – must try harder!*) This organization is reasonably well-intentioned, but it's a case of too many cooks spoiling the broth. There will be a great many people with a great many views, but not many people listening. There will be far too many inconsistent relationships and disconnected initiatives going on, and being seen to do the right things will take precedence over getting results. It could either achieve a lot more or do the same with a lot less. This organization could become a power to be reckoned with if it developed the will to change; however, its problems are deep rooted and will be difficult to overcome. *I'd like to get my teeth into this one.*

4   **Significant competition but short-term window of opportunity.** (*No requirement for fancy customer service.*) Not very effective in a 'Stephen Covey, *Seven Habits*' kind of way, but a formidable force all the same. There will be little unnecessary waste in this organization, which makes a pleasant change: money rules – which is fine. The relationship focus will be strongly upstream, ensuring continuous supply to feed an ever-hungry public. What it lacks in effectiveness it makes up for in efficiency: the boss is likely to drive a Roller, whereas the employees use roller-skates. *An unsung hero of organizational efficiency – don't knock it till you've tried it.*

5   **Monopoly conditions and few long-term aspirations.** (*Money for old rope.*) There is little to motivate people to do a better job here except integrity and personal pride in a job well done. There is often so much work to be done that even the most average performer can get by on leads from *Yellow Pages*. Poor focus and average relationships have proven themselves to be more than sufficient to ease the retirement of a whole generation of plumbers. There will always be a quiet backwater somewhere where the less ambitious can eke out a comfortable living. *Who wants a cup of tea?*

6   **Near monopoly and extreme short-termism.** (*Take the money and run!*) These organizations are about as far away from effective as you can get. One step further and they are a scam! They have few morals and little in the way of efficiency. Relationships – what are they? Their motto is 'if we can get away with it, let's do it'. Often the first into a market, they are usually also the first out. They do have a real eye for spotting a gap and were they to think a bit more long-term, they might make even

more money. These organizations hop from one opportunity to the next, reincarnating themselves to avoid recognition, and are not known for their goodwill or long-term relationships. *Best given a miss by employees, customers and investors alike.*

Fit-for-purpose organizations

In the context of organizations, being good or moral (*à la* Steven Covey) is not always *the most profitable* way forward. Organizations can succeed (at least for a limited time) by short-circuiting the road to morally attuned relationship effectiveness.

People may never get a second chance to make a first impression (unless they are Bill Murray in *Groundhog Day*!), but this is not the case for organizations. Organizations can reinvent themselves repeatedly in a way that people can't legally get away with.

**People are for life – organizations
are for as long as need be.**

Organizations that over-engineer their working culture fail just as fast and just as surely as those that cut too many corners. Organizations can only afford to be fit for the purpose they are designed for – no better, no worse.

Choosing the right working culture is therefore the *big issue* for organizations.

But when it comes to being focused, the picture is slightly different. While there isn't an automatic choice in terms of working culture, there is a natural choice when it comes to focus – being more focused reduces waste and increases profit.

If developing the right working culture is the *big issue* for organizations, being tightly focused is the *big task*!

5.0

The Desire to Amaze

Fine-tuning your aspiration

wjm

Two big steps for organizations

Developing the right working culture and becoming tightly focused are the two top priorities for an organization but, in order to make the right decisions, there are some things we need to know.

- Do differences in the way organizations are owned influence the way they should be run?
- Where do organizations stand in regard to morality and can an organization be immoral?
- Is the concept of service important to an organization's success?
- How should we deal with the issue of job-hopping?
- Should we avoid personality cults?
- What happened to good old-fashioned leadership?
- Are the employees revolting?

To find the answers to these questions and much more, read on!

The question of ownership

Quite a few problems are caused by the relationship between owners and the organizations in which they invest. There are two main types of problem; those caused by owner-managers and those caused when ownership is widely distributed or remote.

The owner-run dilemma

Owner-managers have two separate responsibilities: one as owner and the other as a team member. When they fail to delineate their responsibilities, problems can arise.

Owner-managers have a weakness for making on-the-spot decisions outside of any agreed working culture. The result of this is that other directors feel increasingly unempowered, disenfranchised and unable to make a decision on anything without recourse to the opinions being dispensed by the owner-manager.

This in turn neuters the effectiveness of the whole organization, which is a proven route to chronic Corporate Stress and Corporate Denial.

In my role as relationship troubleshooter, this is a situation that I have personally encountered on many occasions and is the reason why some owner-run organizations stall at success and never make it all the way to amazing success.

PLC problems

When ownership is fragmented, as in some PLCs, directors or others in authority assume the responsibilities of owners and make proxy decisions on their behalf.

Faced with widely distributed ownership and lack of control, directors have a tendency to start treating shareholders' money as if it were their own.

If directors find themselves in a situation where they are not held fully accountable for their behaviour, then every time they wake up in the morning they have to start by thinking, 'Who shall we look after today – us or the shareholders?'

There can be a direct conflict of interest between their responsibility for running an organization and their desire for individual success and pursuit of self-interest.

The situation is exacerbated by the fact that large numbers of small private shareholders are either poorly informed or unable to get their voice heard, and become hostages to the ineffectiveness of the non-executives, institutional investors and quangos that are set up to regulate and influence goings on.

The result of this is that those of us who invest money either directly as shareholders or indirectly through pensions and other institutions, together with members of the taxpaying public, can be taken advantage of.

The companies we invest in and the government departments we depend upon are far less effective than they could be. This is as a direct result of the conflicting personal agendas that obsess many of those whose judgement and endeavour we rely on.

What is more, these issues not only impact on the sharing of the spoils (such as 'fat cat' syndrome), but also directly affect the success of the organizations in meeting their objectives in the first place.

In the absence of more effective methods, directors or department heads are assessed using performance measures substantially dependant on outside influence and vulnerable to manipulation, all of which provide a flawed view of actual competence, endeavour and integrity.

When we consider that those being judged on the results of performance measures are usually also the ones charged with developing, reporting and commentating on them in the first place, the flaws in this system become particularly obvious.

A major rethink of organizational behaviour is needed for both large commercial and large non-commercial organizations, and it is needed now.

If mediocrity is allowed to masquerade as OK, there isn't any incentive for any of this to change. Only by widening the gap between OK and amazing can we make the powers that be sit up and listen.

The moral debate

Where do organizations stand with regards to morality? Can an organization be immoral?

These are important and interesting questions, and in endeavouring to answer them we must remember that life in an organization is not like life at home.

The origin of organizations isn't nest-building; it is the need to work together to feed ourselves and our families.

This is where ideas about organizational leadership have a tendency to go off the rails. We can be easily seduced by a view of the world where nice people always win, bosses are warm and loving, employees respond by being honest and hard working, and customers always tell the truth.

But unfortunately this is not always the case!

In the real world:

- people are a mixed bag of personalities and characters; and
- business is governed by survival of the fittest.

The organizational playing field is not a picnic or a school outing but an arena where we must win at the expense of the competition.

And when big money is the main goal, organizational performance is usually at its keenest! This means that:

Successful profit-orientated organizations are usually amoral, opportunity-converting money machines!

When we use terms such as 'moral' and 'amoral', we need to be careful: they are significant words laden with hidden and complex meanings. Because of this I have decided to explain how I am using them in the context of this book.

- Morality: the existence of standards of conduct that are accepted as right and proper, and judging the rightness or wrongness of everything by these standards.
- Moral: using one's personal conscience to determine what is right and wrong regardless of laws or situations, and drawing conclusions on how to behave from one's own personal beliefs.
- Amoral: not susceptible to personal moral judgements.
- Immoral: contrary to accepted moral principles.

Organizations, however, are more like machines than people.

An organization's success is dependent on its ability to consistently replicate successful behaviour and consistent relationships.

Look at it this way:

- a gun is judged to be a success if it is effective at killing people and not by whether it knows who to shoot – that is the responsibility of the person firing it;
- an army is victorious when it wins and not for the reasons it is fighting – that is the role of politicians; and
- a hyena succeeds and goes on to breed when it kills or scavenges enough prey, and not by whether it plays fair or not – that is for God to decide.

Successful organizations can be amoral; that is, not susceptible to personal moral judgements:

- they can succeed regardless of whether they are in the arms industry, selling tobacco or finding cures for deadly diseases;
- they have no existential reason to exist – they are not human and they are not created by God in his own image;
- they know no good and bad, only success and failure; and
- they do not need to abide by human morality – there is no question of them going to Heaven.

A successful organization must be consistently ruthless in line with stated principles, in the pursuit of stated goals.

Everybody within a successful organization must understand exactly what standards of behaviour are expected from them based on a clear working culture and must not draw separate conclusions based on their own individual social paradigms.

> **Total consistent focus makes for a successful organization – not the use of good intentions.**

This does not change whether the organization is Save the Children, the Inland Revenue or a car-clamping firm.

> **Failing organizations are morally confused and contradictory – they have no clear standards of conduct.**

Creating a working culture is not a random act and everyone within an organization must adhere to it.

When individuals work outside of an agreed working culture by declaring independence and doing their own thing it leads to wasted resources, organizational stress, strained relationships and ultimately failure.

Being poorly focused makes an organization perform poorly. Different directors using their own ideas to make decisions rather than following a single working culture causes great harm. Equally, when directors go in one direction and employees go in another, it is a recipe for waste and disaster.

Any organization that rejects the idea of a single working culture is in a state of anarchy and will be unable to function as a single entity. This type of organization is actually a loosely connected group of separate people pursuing individual relationships and not an organization at all.

It is unable to take corporate or organizational responsibility, will pursue separate agendas and be inconsistent in its actions.

The concept of service

How important is the concept of service to an organization's success? What is the most effective working culture for any organization looking to foster amazingly successful relationships?

As we have seen, one key issue is how long we are planning on being in town. If all we want to do is make a quick buck and move on, there is absolutely no point spending a single penny we don't absolutely need to.

But that is not the route to creating an amazingly successful organization.

The only approach for an organization to take if it wants to become amazingly successful is to become highly effective and highly focused.

And that doesn't pay dividends overnight.

But no single working culture is right for every situation. If I use the analogy of a car, different working cultures deliver different rates of acceleration and different top speeds.

Why should anyone spend money to create a future that they do not expect to be part of?

Why invest in intangible assets that are hard to value on the balance sheet such as staff, improving team moral, developing customer focus and lifting competence levels, if you expect to be moving on soon?

This is, after all, the age of the disposable organization!

Despite all of this, a working culture centred around the concept of service generally and customer service specifically is the most likely to deliver long-term amazing success.

An organization that wants to adopt a service-based working culture must however be ready for the long haul.

It must have both the patience and the resources to get through the early stages in a market where market dominance and being the largest are critical whatever the future price.

> **Service-based working cultures deliver far more but deliver it more slowly.**

Will the competitive nature of the market you are operating in allow you the luxury of doing all the right things?

Some organizations are better off starting with one working culture and then migrating to another when scale and success allow or demand it.

Planning to evolve or change our working culture is fine as an idea when those in charge are sufficiently switched on to the challenges of changing an organization's culture: to act at the appropriate time and effectively instigate a culture shift in line with new market conditions.

But let's not forget that the larger an organization is, the more careful it must be in choosing its working culture in the first instance. Larger organizations are always going to be harder to change; they are clumsy and less fleet of foot than their smaller counterparts. Larger organizations must change their working culture less often and less dramatically, so must put more time and effort into avoiding problems in the first place.

Coping with job-hopping

There is an increasing tendency for both employees and organizational leaders to shed companies the way insects shed skins.

Jobs are no longer for life, and people are learning to adopt and discard working cultures as fast as teenagers change their boyfriends or girlfriends. As a result we are starting to treat working cultures as if they are an outfit we wear for work and then discard at the end of the day.

This works reasonably well in retail outlets or call centres, where staff are expected to operate within agreed customer service procedures and the working culture is simply a model they follow in fulfilling their job. However, it wears incredibly thin when leaders of organizations treat working culture in the same way.

Every member of a leadership team needs to be closely involved with the working culture they are at least partly responsible for. They need to understand all possible nuances and implications, as they are responsible for applying it to many more complex business scenarios than those of their admin or call centre staff.

When senior managers change jobs, they are likely – for a time, at least – to retain elements of their old working culture, and the more senior a person is when they join an organization the more this will happen. If they were comfortable with their old working culture they will resist changing it regardless of any organizational pressure they may experience.

This is one of the reasons why many executives who take up senior positions from outside an organization fail to settle down and end up moving on.

Forcing out newly arrived senior managers this way may be essential to the continuing harmony of an organization. On the other hand, it may be an example of the organization's failure to recognize the need for change and could well be a reason for stalled success.

Personality cults

In the absence of an agreed working culture the leaders of an organization will use their own personalities to dictate the way relationships are handled in their own area of influence.

The relative power and influence of each member of the leadership team will determine the relative strength of their cultural influence. Whatever the relative balance, however, you can be absolutely certain that this will create confusion, waste and stress.

The result will be a cult of personality with the more dominant leaders commanding more followers, resulting in a split working culture within the organization.

It is interesting to note that when individual people suffer from a split or multiple personality they are usually diagnosed as schizophrenic and receive the benefit of medical help. When organizations suffer from a split or multiple culture, it is usually accepted as normal.

The effect of this can be seen in the way organizations respond differently to sales enquiries than to service enquiries.

How many times have you been left to wonder alone in a shop because a sales assistant is suddenly needed elsewhere when they discover that you are only enquiring, and not intending to buy there and then?

How many organizations have you encountered that are happy to answer a sales enquiry with a live person answering after one ring on a freephone number, but leave existing customers in an automated answering system, costing them a fortune in phone charges? (My personal tip here is to ring the sales line and make them transfer you!)

This type of totally inconsistent and unacceptable behaviour is still, I am afraid, commonplace, and explains why many companies are destined to reside in corporate limbo unless someone takes action.

Clear, concise demonstration

Happily, for every organization that is struggling with job-hopping and the signs of a multiple working culture, there is another forging ahead in a single-minded way.

A key lesson I have learnt from observing people is that regardless of what approach we take, it is the force with which we take it with that counts:

- if you want to be good, be a saint; and
- if you are going to be a bastard, be a complete bastard.

People who run successful organizations are incredibly driven and are ruthless in pursuit of their goals.

They exhibit the same behaviours regardless of whether they are a missionary in Africa, a school head teacher, a second-hand car dealer or even an estate agent – *all that varies is the working culture they work within*.

Following this logic, it seems reasonable to expect that leaders of successful organizations should share some common traits and that these should be related to success rather than purpose.

Having discussed this at length with my colleagues and having analyzed the behaviour of people who I considered to be in this category, certain consistent traits have become clear.

In our experience, successful leaders clearly, consistently and concisely demonstrate the principles and priorities they want their organization to adhere to in the way they personally behave; in effect, they live the working culture they want the organization to follow.

Heads of successful organizations:

- personify the organizations they represent;
- separate their operational and institutional responsibilities;
- are so equated with the purpose of the organization that they can describe it fluidly without pausing for a breath;
- use agreed criteria to decide what is important and what is a potential distraction;
- communicate concisely but with passion;
- possess infectious enthusiasm but do not let their own personality become more important than the organization or the message;
- control the behaviour of their organizations and abide by the agreed working culture themselves; and
- prioritize the importance of consistent relationships.

Personal demonstration by a leader of an organization's working culture is so important that it is hard to imagine an organization really succeeding without it.

Good old-fashioned leadership is alive and well!

Not only are consistent relationships and clear, concise demonstration of purpose and principles vital to leaders, they are also vital to everyone in the organization: nothing should be lost in translation.

Everyone must deliver the same messages, not only in what they say but also in the way they behave.

Amazing success can be viewed like this:

$$\text{Being clear} + \text{Being concise} + \text{Personal demonstration} \times \text{Everyone} = \text{Ongoing success}$$

The employees are revolting

Nothing matters if, at the end of the day, the employees of an organization either reject outright – or, as is more common, fight a rearguard action against – an organization's working culture.

And believe me, although this may be the last fence, it is frightening how many organizations fall at it.

There are several reasons why this might happen.

The adoption process was flawed

You can't dump a working culture on an organization and expect endless thanks: the way it is introduced will be critical to its success. Employees must be gently wooed and made to feel a fully contributing part of any development.

Many organizations put in only a fraction of the effort required to do this job properly, which is why many working cultures are never effectively picked up by the entire organization.

Effective organizations are starting to contemplate employing the art of theatre and the development of corporate rituals, recognizing that as the standard of communication in the entertainment and leisure industries rise, so must the standard of communication at work.

With shorter concentration spans and reduced loyalty on one hand and increasing expectations and choice on the other, only organizations that take selling their cultures seriously are likely to prosper in the future.

No incentives were included

How many directors do you know who are willing to change their behaviour without having a good reason to do so? Not many, I suspect!

Yet this does not stop organizations trying to change employee behaviour without making it worthwhile for all involved.

For too long, corporate remuneration and incentives have either played against or have not helped organizations to achieve behavioural goals. Many have been based on financial or performance-related targets that have had the spin-off of actually encouraging antisocial or damaging behaviour.

Some other bonus schemes are not actually based on anything significant and like lift music get lost in the background, having little or no effect yet still costing large amounts of money!

A new mindset is required where reward is based on desired behaviour as well as performance.

No penalties were clear

This must go hand in glove with the point above. A working culture should form a mutually binding contract between the organization and everyone who works in it.

Every working culture needs a transparent and fair review process, and those that deliberately infringe the rules must be held to account for it.

There cannot be one rule for the goose and another for the gander. Those in charge must allow themselves to be reviewed and rewarded in the same clear, open manner that applies to everyone else.

Justice cannot be the prerogative of the few: whatever the system, someone must have the guts to make it work. One criticism of British managers is that although they talk a good game, when push comes to shove they would rather duck the hard issues of discipline.

Much of society today is so concerned with political correctness that people prefer to overlook unacceptable behaviour rather than be in danger of becoming known as the office bully!

But the problem is, if one person is seen to get away with poor behaviour then there is little incentive for others to do what is expected of them.

The employees don't like what they hear

We all have free will and if you try to implement a working culture that employees don't like or agree with, you are going to have a fight on your hands.

If people are resistant to the way we want them to behave or if they feel they are badly prepared or trained, they will find a million and one ways of frustrating us. Rather than saying no, they will shrink away from what we want them to do at every opportunity.

Organizations are adept at the tactics of guerrilla warfare: it is more like facing an internal resistance movement or, in extreme cases, a terrorist group, than fighting a traditional war. They will not face you in the open but will retreat, regroup and hit back in a thousand different ways.

The only workable solution is discussion and compromise on both sides. It may well be that important points have been missed and that addressing these issues will improve the performance of the whole organization.

The working culture is undermined by the personal behaviour of the leadership team

This is probably the greatest killer of a working culture that there is.

There is a natural assumption that comes with the gaining of power: that as a senior manager, we are free to do things that other employees would be fired for! Somehow, as senior managers, we often seem to think we are above the laws of the organization.

Very few of us, if we are honest, can say that this has never crossed our mind, but the bare-faced cheek of some directors willing to say one thing and do another is almost beyond the bounds of comprehension.

Do they think that everyone else is stupid or does not care?

On occasions it borders on the attitude that saw Charles I lose his head – and what did not suit a king is particularly ill-suited to your average bureaucrat.

This type of behaviour is the kiss of death for any working culture and is a sure sign of Corporate Denial.

6.0

Corporate Evolution

Why some organizations grow up faster and stronger

wjm

Growing up

Organizations, as we know, are not conscious in the same way people are: they do not have their own memory and the future can be separated from the past more quickly and totally.

The way organizations learn, store and share knowledge becomes key, and any effective organization must encourage learning. It must always be able to learn and store the lessons of the past, but with people coming and going faster and faster, this is not always easy.

At the same time as learning fast and remembering important lessons, they must also be able to *unlearn* and break bad habits, which can be a more difficult task than effective learning.

Every new organizational generation must be given a fresh chance to prove itself.

As chairmen and CEOs come and go, so the organizational slate can be wiped clean in the same way that the sins of the father should not be passed on to the son. Organizations need to choose wisely about what to hang on to and what to jettison.

Evolution versus change

Change is a cornerstone of any organization, regardless of how successful it currently is. But change will always be, at least to some extent, a painful and risky experience.

Effective change involves making sacrifices today in the expectation of future gains. A willingness to compromise and make certain sacrifices is also a cornerstone of long-lasting relationships.

These are the essential ingredients of organizational evolution and without them, change becomes a directionless end in itself, resulting not in evolution, but in constant, confusing change.

But there is never any reason to expect evolution to be easy: many organizations disagree about current priorities, let alone future ones, and the concept of sacrifice in any form can often be a taboo subject altogether!

So what do we know about the concept of corporate evolution?

I have identified four levels of organizational evolution, although there is no indication that these need be passed through sequentially. Indeed, the evidence shows that the more direct the evolutionary path, the greater the chances of strong relationships and an amazingly successful organization.

The four levels of organizational evolution are:

- Primitive
- Mercenary
- Feudal
- Advanced.

Primitive Organizations

Primitive Organizations exhibit all the classic features of any start-up. Energy and anticipation are usually high and the right start-up can almost run on pure adrenalin.

Primitive Organizations naturally perform the things that other types of organizations have to work hard to achieve. Formal structure and communication is not yet necessary, as enthusiasm and team spirit can carry the organization along.

In the early stages most Primitive Organizations manage to operate under one working culture and build effective internal and external relationships. This state of affairs can't last, however, as Primitive Organizations are naturally transient. When the initial honeymoon period passes, the culture of the organization will change of its own accord.

All that is up for debate is how much it will change, how fast it will change and whether that change will be managed or if nature will be allowed to take its own course.

As is the case with all organizations, Primitive Organizations face the choice of managing their culture from the word go, or leaving it to chance. Unfortunately too many organizations rely on the natural spirit associated with being a Primitive start-up and de-prioritize cultural investment, choosing to concentrate on what they see as operational necessities.

To a point this is understandable, but I believe this attitude reflects some common misconceptions.

- An organization's honeymoon period or Primitive stage can be incredibly short, which catches a lot of organizations out – and once the damage is done, it's done. Remedial work is always harder and significantly more draining and time-consuming than proactive effort.
- Proactive cultural and relationship management right from the start can be achieved at minimal cost in terms of time and money, and will deliver benefit for years to come. It is worth remembering that managing a working culture does not mean over-engineering it: in fact, it should mean quite the opposite.

Even in start-ups, Corporate Stress and embryonic Corporate Denial will cost an organization far more dearly than the cost of proactive culture and relationship management.

Good practice from day one is what creates long-term amazing relationships and long-term success.

Mercenary Organizations

Mercenary Organizations have moved on from the Primitive start-up stage. They have established infrastructure, need good internal communication to achieve what Primitive Organizations achieve naturally and will have developed strategies to motivate people.

Without proactive relationship and culture management, many Mercenary Organizations will end up operating more than one working culture and lose focus as a result. Stress can only build, relationships suffer and Corporate Denial becomes a real prospect.

Any failure to institutionalize mutually trusting relationships during the Primitive stage will now take its toll. The transactional relationships that are the bedrock of Mercenary Organizations work fine from an economic perspective but build little if any trust.

Without trust there is no loyalty and without loyalty, internal division and stand-offs will be unavoidable. Meanwhile, customer and supplier relationships will tend to be skin deep.

It is hard for any organization that is not trust-based to pretend it is when dealing with outside parties: too many obvious inconsistencies will come to the surface as different managers and staff represent the organization in different ways, and conflicting corporate policies, marketing initiatives and poor service will let the organization down.

Feudal Organizations

Feudal Organizations are a step beyond Mercenary, brought about by advancing tension, stress and divisions.

In Feudal Organizations there are clear separate camps, divided loyalties, multiple working cultures, damaged relationships and usually substantial waste. Corporate Denial will be unavoidable.

Feudal Organizations are a cost of failure on the part of their management teams. They are also often the result of unfair or overly protected market conditions. These organizations do things because they can: there is little if any attempt to change and bad practice is accepted as OK.

Anyone from the leadership team of a Feudal Organization that is reading this will think I am either mad, bad, both or not talking about them. There are none as blind as those that do not wish to see.

Advanced Organizations

Advanced Organizations are the highest level of organizational evolution. They will posses a strong service-based working culture and represent the height of organizational maturity.

Gone are the divisions common to both Feudal and Mercenary Organizations, replaced instead by harmony, focus and consistent relationships.

Advanced Organizations are destined to be the most stable and longest-lived of all. They invest heavily in relationships, build trust with all parties and act with integrity.

The secret to becoming an Advanced Organization lies in a smooth transition straight from Primitive to Advanced, missing out the distractions and pitfalls of Mercenary and Feudal existence, and is achieved through proactive relationship and culture management from the very beginning.

The process of organizational evolution

This process is illustrated in Figure 6.1.

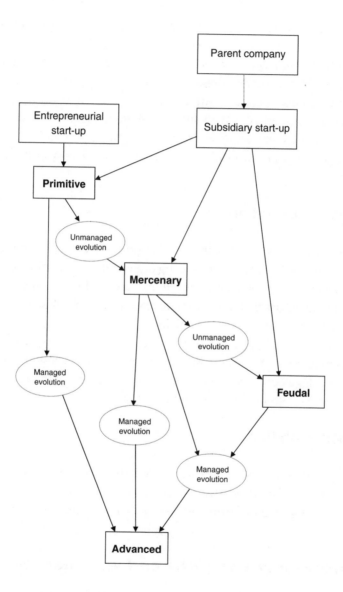

Fig 6.1   The process of organizational evolution

Start-up organizations

Organizational start-ups usually take one of two forms:

- entrepreneurial start-ups – fresh ventures set up as independent entities; and
- subsidiary start-ups – as offshoots of existing organizations both commercial and public, these often inherit the working culture of the parent organization and may bypass Primitive and move straight to Mercenary or Feudal. Given sufficient independence, they can become a Primitive Organization in their own right but are unlikely to move straight to Advanced, as this requires trust that can only be built up over time.

Unmanaged evolution

If the leadership team of any start-up takes no positive steps to control their cultural future, the fate of any burgeoning organization will be in the lap of the gods. Proactive relationship and culture management is the only way for an organization to ensure that it does not develop a multiple or split culture and set itself on the road to stress and Denial.

Feudal Organizations will find it extremely hard to change without clear and strenuous action to reverse the trends of the past. These organizations have usually developed deep-seated cultural divides and nothing will change without positive restorative and remedial action.

Managed evolution

Managed evolution is the only way for organizations to control their own destiny and can take one of two forms which can involve the use of either Relationship Mapping or Truth and Reconciliation, which will be described shortly.

Organizational strengths and weaknesses

How different is each level of organizational evolution? And what benefits and downsides does each level bring with it?

So that we can compare each level on an equal footing I have taken six headings and analyzed each one.

The six headings are:

- philosophy
- motivation
- focus
- confidence
- timescale
- strengths.

Major differences are soon easy to spot!

Philosophy

Primitive	**Mercenary**	**Feudal**	**Advanced**
Sowing	Exploitation	Taxing	Harvesting

The basic philosophies behind the main organizational levels could not be more different.

Primitive Organizations are at the beginning of the cycle, as would be expected, and their philosophy is centred around sowing today so they can reap tomorrow. They recognize that without the hard graft of preparing the land there can be no returns, and are prepared to invest time and money now in the belief that returns will follow. They share the spirit of any adventurers, such as the pioneers who went west in search of new land and opportunity in the American West.

This is frontiersville!

Mercenaries have clearly moved on and are in the realm of exploiting opportunities: hunting, fishing and mining is a fair description of their philosophy. Mercenaries are looking for an immediate return on energy expended and are not in the business of long-term investment.

The philosophy of Feudal Organizations is another clear step on from mercenaries and is focused on the concept of taxing the hard work, endeavour and risk-taking of others. Where mercenaries were looking for immediate returns it was at least as the result of their own efforts; Feudal Organizations believe in immediate returns off the back of other people's efforts or through taking advantage of lack of customer choice.

Exploitation of resources is at the heart of Mercenary Organizations, whereas exploiting other people is the central theme of the Feudal philosophy. Stakeholders, customers and employees can all be fair game to a Feudal Organization.

With Advanced Organizations, we see another philosophy come into play. Advanced Organizations are built around the concept of harvesting: they understand that there is a natural cycle to life and are committed to following that cycle. They have the patience to sow, tend the crops and expect a good harvest. They know that harvests will by nature vary and plan over a longer term, expecting good and bad results to be evened out.

They also understand the concept of celebration and of harvest festivals. Ritual and its significance to the lives of individuals is taken into account, and reflected in the way the organization operates.

Motivation

Primitive	**Mercenary**	**Feudal**	**Advanced**
Idea-based	Knowledge-based	Power-based	Trust-based

Ideas are without doubt the oxygen of the Primitive Organization. Innovation, invention and hot-housing are all vital: without ideas and passion, there is no hope for a Primitive Organization.

As an organization grows in both success and size, the emphasis shifts from pure ideas to knowledge. Knowledge management becomes key and the ability to process information and deduce the right outcomes is vital. With greater amounts of knowledge spread over an increasingly large base, the role of communication also becomes pivotal.

Feudal Organizations are not rooted in fairness or equality so rely on power-based implementation. Hierarchy, enforcement and bullying are all seen as fair game.

The most remarkable aspect of Advanced Organizations is their ability to generate trust amongst employees and customers alike. This is built upon adherence to the truth and an understanding of the importance of doing what the organization says it will do. Advanced Organizations are able to use their trust base to great advantage in virtually every aspect of their business relationships.

Focus

Primitive	Mercenary	Feudal	Advanced
External	External	Internal	Internal and external

Both Primitive and Mercenary Organizations are heavily externally focused, even if it is for slightly different reasons. If either type of organization takes its eye off the market place then it is in trouble.

Feudal Organizations, on the other hand, feel no such compunction; since they usually operate in a protected market place in the first place, they are far more wrapped up in their own internal machinations.

Internal agendas and self-justification are way up the list of importance and this becomes even more marked when Feudal Organizations are clustered together – in the EU, for example. Each organization has a self-fulfilling effect on each of the others, allowing them to coexist in their own little private fantasy land – all, of course, funded by us!

Advanced Organizations are nicely balanced, recognizing the obvious importance of the market place but also recognizing the importance of refreshing and investing in their own organization to keep it healthy.

Confidence

Primitive	Mercenary	Feudal	Advanced
Shared confidence	Self-confidence	Low self-esteem	Quietly confident

Mutual support and shared confidence are vital to any Primitive Organization. Without the back-up of each other, life in a Primitive Organization can be unbearably hard. Self-belief is essential and without shared confidence this cannot be maintained.

In Mercenary Organizations this goes a stage further and self-belief becomes self-confidence. There is only a thin line between self-confidence and arrogance, which is why Mercenary Organizations have to tread very carefully in all their relationships.

As with many bullies, Feudal Organizations have low self-esteem – which explains much of their behaviour. With a bit more confidence they would spend less time hiding behind barriers of one sort or another and would end up running far better businesses.

Advanced Organizations take more of a cue from Mercenary Organizations but replace self-confidence with quiet confidence. Advanced Organizations are experienced and assured: they are the type of organization that doesn't have to try too hard.

Timescales

Primitive	Mercenary	Feudal	Advanced
Short term	Medium term	Medium term	Long term

Primitive Organizations are not by nature sustainable. These are the teenagers of organizations, developing their individuality, flexing their muscles and testing their pulling power with those whose attention they are seeking to attract. If they don't grow up they have a problem: the sort of things that a teenage girl can get away are ill-suited to a middle-aged woman.

Mercenary and Feudal Organizations are usually medium term. Their longevity will depend on the market conditions they operate in and their ability to reinvent themselves. It can appear more appealing to an organization to continually reinvent itself than bother to mature.

Advanced Organizations are the only truly long-term, long-lasting organizations. Their balance and banks of trust allow them to survive and grow when others will fall by the wayside.

Strengths

Primitive	Mercenary	Feudal	Advanced
Hope	Negotiation	Regulation	Demonstration
Energy	Financial control	Supply management	Consensus
Innovation	Branding efficiency	Administration	Trust
		Control systems	Track record
			Self-control
			Relationships

Primitive Organizations are masters at harnessing hope, energy and innovation. These are the most spirited organizations and can drive themselves forward in a way that even Advanced Organizations would find extremely hard.

Mercenary Organizations have to be more organized as they are usually far bigger and more complicated. They are often the best branded organizations and are tightly run from a financial point of view.

Feudal Organizations take things a stage further again and use their propensity for paranoia as a catalyst for focusing on control systems. With little trust around, they believe that if something is not tied down then some toe-rag will try and steal it. The ability of this type of organization to measure and record almost everything is remarkable; it is only a shame that the few things they don't normally measure relate to their own performance and customer satisfaction.

Advanced Organizations put enormous store by demonstration, both at a personal level and at a corporate level. Being seen to do the right thing is taken seriously, as the importance of a consistently strong track record is never lost to them.

Consensus and self-control are also strengths. Unlike many organizations that desperately try to defend self-regulation as a satisfactory market control, these are organizations that actually could self-regulate themselves and behave with complete corporate responsibility as well. Strong relationships are a way of life.

Testing relationships

Here is a simple test that can be applied to any organization to find out how strong its relationship base is and whether the organization is likely to be Primitive, Mercenary, Feudal or Advanced.

There are ten key relationship indicators, five positive and five negative. Each indicator can be applied to all organizational relationships.

The positive relationship indicators are:

- respect – relationships based on mutual respect;
- transparency – relationships based on openness and transparency;
- trust – significant trust between all parties;
- reputation – reputation for fair dealing; and
- delegation – effective delegation based on clear expectations.

The negative indicators are:

- coercion – coercion as a basis for action;
- image – over-reliance on image rather than substance;
- manipulation – manipulation of facts or people to gain an unfair advantage;
- bribery – reliance on pure financial reward and personal gain as key motivators; and
- regulation – reliance on regulation to defend a position.

When any of the first five indicators is believed to be present, the organization scores one point. When any of the second five indicators are present, a point should be deducted.

When these indicators are applied to the key organizational types described earlier, a picture emerges that clearly reflects the strength of the relationship base of each organizational type (see Table 6.1)

Negative scores indicate that an organization is either Feudal or currently Mercenary but with the propensity to become Feudal. Scores around zero are likely to indicate a Mercenary Organization and a score from two to three indicates that an organization is likely to be Primitive or in a state of transition. Any score of four or above indicates an Advanced Organization.

Table 6.1

Indicator	Primitive	Mercenary	Feudal	Advanced
Positive				
Reputation				*
Respect	*	*		*
Transparency	*			*
Trust	*			*
Delegation	*	*		*
Score	+4	+2	-	+5
Negative				
Coercion			*	
Image		*		
Manipulation			*	
Bribery	*	*	*	
Regulation			*	
Score	-1	-2	-4	-
Total Score	+3	-	-4	+5

7.0

Truth and Reconciliation in Business

How to break with the past and move on

wjm

Hearing the truth

There are times in the life of most companies when something special and extraordinary is needed to break the monotony of ordinary, feed starving relationships and encourage not small steps but giant leaps forward.

> *'Courage is what it takes to stand up and speak … courage is also what it takes to sit down and listen.'*
>
> Winston Churchill

These are the times when personal courage is needed and, as Winston Churchill said, not only the courage to stand up and be heard, but also the courage to sit down and listen to some hard truths.

At these times an organization should consider engaging in Truth and Reconciliation in Business.

Organizations in the depth of Denial and confounded by chronic Corporate Stress are not going to be able to wake up one morning and forget the past and just start again. These organizations are going to need a healing process to become fit and healthy.

As in personal relationships their problems will be deep rooted: any superficial treatment is doomed to failure. Individuals experiencing relationship crisis are usually unable to be sufficiently objective to sort out their own problems, which is why they call on the services of relationship counselling services such as Relate.

Relate takes a dispassionate stance and allows both parties, often for the first time in years, to actually hear what the other is saying. Only through this process of listening and accepting in a supportive, objective environment can change and progress start to take place.

It is exactly the same for organizations – only a thousand times worse, because instead of two voices needing to be heard there may be tens, hundreds or even thousands to be taken into account.

Recognising the scale of resentment that builds up in organizations and the scale of the numbers involved, I looked around at other models for reconciling differences that might be useful in helping organizations change and develop their culture.

I started to look at the truth and reconciliation committees that have been set up in numerous countries around the world, including Chile, South Africa and the former Yugoslavia. The scale of the atrocities that these committees were set up to deal with is of course incomparable to anything requiring attention in even the worst commercial organization. These committees dealt with murder, torture, rape and the very worst crimes imaginable, but the point is this: if the approach they took worked in those appalling situations then the principles must be right, if used appropriately, for a whole variety of less serious situations.

Just as organizations can learn from the methods of relationship counselling, so they can also learn from the methods of truth and reconciliation committees.

As a result of my research and after trials with organizations of different sizes, I have stripped out what I think are the appropriate principles of truth and reconciliation and married them to the methods of relationship counselling to create Truth and Reconciliation in Business.

Truth and Reconciliation in Business is a thorough and rigorous solution to eradicating chronic Corporate Stress and Corporate Denial. It does not skim over the surface, it does not cure symptoms while ignoring root causes and it does not paper over cracks.

It confronts problems, it gets to the truth and fosters acceptance of the real condition of an organization, it is not punitive or unnecessarily judgemental and it is not looking to blame or punish.

It seeks to establish a firm and sustainable base from which an organization can move on effectively and – using the next stage of the rebuilding process, Relationship Mapping – establish amazing relationships with all its constituent parts.

Truth and Reconciliation in Business is an extremely human experience where the emphasis is on truth, dialogue and understanding rather than strict adherence to a tightly defined auditable process.

Success or failure of the exercise will depend on the spirit and willingness with which each party engages and the desire of every party to contribute to building a better future for the organization.

And like all journeys, it starts with a single step!

Coming out

Who can act to confront Corporate Denial or help an organization in need of relationship support?

The short answer to this is that in theory anyone can.

Remember the old phrase 'the revolution will not be televised'? The impetus for change can come from anywhere but must be pulled together to form a nucleus. That nucleus is likely to form around a key individual within the organization with the will-power and strength of character to challenge the status quo.

Engaging in Truth and Reconciliation in Business requires an admission that all is not well, and this can be hard for anyone. Individuals respond to this type of situation with a mixture of guilt and aggression based on insecurity about their personal situation and a suspicion of personal inadequacy about being able to perform any better.

This is totally normal and must be dealt with. It is a key requirement of anyone sponsoring Truth and Reconciliation in Business that they are able to help others cope with and overcome any worry that the process might uncover their personal inadequacies.

Corporate Denial and the behaviours associated with it are the result of a systematic breakdown of organizational standards. They are not the result of one individual's failings, however much it might feel that way; relationships degenerate because a series of relationships collapses one after another and eventually breaks down the culture of an organization.

Any individual who takes it upon themselves to turn this around must be prepared to sing out of tune and, for a time at least, be the lone voice in the choir.

As anyone who has dealt with the victims of abusive relationships will know, the victims often end up blaming themselves for everything that is going wrong. This happens in organizations as well. Any Truth and Reconciliation in Business champion must be prepared for this and make it clear from the outset that the exercise is not about blame allocation but about breaking the habits and relationships of the past to build a brighter better future.

The greatest problem that I have ever had to overcome whilst working in organizations is not recognizing problems or developing workable solutions; it is helping someone find the courage to do something about it, overcome their own fears and have the skill to stop others in their tracks, making them see the reality of life as it really is.

During one meeting I was discussing this issue with a client and he suddenly looked up and said, 'The problem we have here is not proving we have a problem because we all know that – it is getting the MD to come out of the closet! To stand up and say this is a dysfunctional organization and let's all do something about it.'

And he was absolutely right!

After this I changed my approach to working with companies. I stopped focusing on the problems, which were largely self-evident to those that wanted to see them, and I stopped focusing on the solutions, because those were not rocket science either.

Where I have focused since is giving people the courage to speak out and the skills to convince others of the need for action.

Helping people to turn up the volume and silence the room with their passion for a better future and their unarguable confidence that a better future can collectively be achieved is the critical challenge.

> **Giving people the confidence to say, 'We are in Denial but I am going to do something about it!'**

Understanding Truth and Reconciliation in Business

'… there is a right to know the truth contained within the right to seek, receive and impart information.'

The Universal Declaration of Human Rights, article 19

Access to the truth is a fundamental human right and as such it must form the foundation of any truly amazing organization capable of maintaining long-term, mutually respectful and beneficial relationships. As Jonathan Ball says:

> **Without truth there can be no trust, without trust there can be no peace and without peace there can be no prosperity.**

This is as true of organizations as it is of nation states or families.

Truth and Reconciliation in Business aims to achieve exactly what it says. It aims to get to the truth about the way relationships are being conducted and it aims to use the acceptance of that truth as the basis for reconciling the organization and building fresh new relationships.

There is a great quote by Albie Sachs, who was a judge on South Africa's Constitutional Court, that highlights the issues that organizations face when striving to develop more constructive relationships between their leadership team, management, employees generally, customers, shareholders and the society and environment in which the organization operates.

This quote reads:

> *'If we wanted our common citizenship to be worth anything we had to overcome the practice of having a white history and a black history, resulting in two completely separate and unrecognized accounts of what happened in our country; we needed all to be on the same existential map for the first time, to cease once and for all being settlers and natives with different and incompatible destinies.*
>
> *'This required not simply decontextualized, static, accurately focused microscopic truths, but broadly located, mobile, multi-layered and interactive truth.'*
>
> *The Soft Vengeance of a Freedom Fighter*, Albie Sachs, 2000

Replace 'white and black' and 'settlers and natives' with 'management and employees' and substitute 'country' with 'organization' and what Albie Sachs is saying with regard to South Africa is directly applicable to many organizations.

In the context of organizations, the Albie Sachs quote can be read this way:

> *'If we want our organization to be amazingly successful we must confront and overcome the practice of having completely separate management, employee and stakeholder perspectives, dividing the way we see our organization's current and future priorities.*
>
> *'We need to develop one working culture capable of uniting our unreconciled and incompatible aspirations and goals.*
>
> *'This requires us to focus not only on our systems and processes but to*

build strong, dynamic relationships based on dialogue, interaction, genuinely shared values, mutual respect, inclusiveness, openness and trust.'

Coming to terms with this challenge is one of the greatest opportunities facing organizations today and the only way to beat Corporate Denial, the world's most damaging business taboo!

In the words of the *New York Times*:

> *'True reconciliation, which occurs when a society is no longer paralyzed by the past and people can work together, cannot be based on silence.'*
>
> 1 November 1998

Truth and reconciliation, as practised by nation states such as South Africa, is a detailed process used under the most extreme situations – far removed from anything I or indeed any of us has probably seen in any organization.

But let's not miss the lessons these experiences can teach us about unity and strength, and about how to create harmony in inharmonious situations.

Truth and Reconciliation in Business is a significantly scaled-down version with reduced scope based on a drastically reduced need. What it does do, however, is adhere to principles proven in the most extreme environments where demands for forgiveness take on monumental proportions.

The stages of Truth and Reconciliation in Business

There are four key stages to Truth and Reconciliation in Business:

- Acceptance and recognition;
- Seeking the truth;
- Acting consistently and decisively; and
- Preventing repetition.

Acceptance and recognition

Acceptance and recognition are two different but connected things, acceptance of the need to act and a willingness to play a part in reconciling problems being one part. This can only happen after there has first been a genuine recognition of the problems by all concerned.

All parties within an organization should play their part in this process and the transparency, openness and neutrality of proceedings are all critical to success.

Regular open and honest communication and feedback are as important as inclusiveness. Truths that everyone knows to be true but are not openly accepted must not only be accepted but must be publicly recognized as true. Failure to openly recognize these things will damage the credibility of those in authority and, indeed, the credibility of the whole process.

This is not a process to be entered into frivolously: integrity and determination will be needed to progress the process through to the type of conclusion that is capable of turning a whole organization on its head, creating a new working culture, new relationships and launching it on the path to becoming an Advanced Organization and ultimately amazingly successful.

Indeed, determination will be needed in no small measure just to get acceptance and recognition moving in the first place.

I object!

Objections are the natural response to any attempt to transform an organization's culture and relationships, and must be expected and overcome. Any Truth and Reconciliation in Business champion can expect to have to overcome numerous objections.

'We are sort of doing this already'

Yeah right! People will claim that things are not that bad and that similar approaches are already in action. This is usually Denial at its naked best. Comparing some loosely engaged change initiative to Truth and Reconciliation in Business, toughly implemented, is like comparing plastic to platinum.

'If it was just up to me I'd do it straight away'

Anybody can start the revolution and it is up to everyone to take responsibility for playing their part in raising the organization's aspirations and making OK a thing of the past.

'We've tried this stuff before and it didn't work'

Sometimes in life you have to kiss a few frogs! Truth and Reconciliation in Business is based on ideas that have been proven in some of the most testing arenas in the world. This process only fails when badly implemented, and that is a promise.

'No one wants to hear the truth'

First get to the truth and then we can start to deal with it. A lot of people do not want to hear this stuff; a lot of people are happy with an ordinary, second division performance. The question is, are you?

'This type of thing causes as many problems as it solves'

Facing up to reality doesn't create problems – it only confronts problems that already exist.

'We really want to do this but the timing is not quite right'

When will the timing be right? Probably never or too late to help is the usual answer. There is no such thing as a perfect time, but timing can only ever get worse. The more Corporate Denial is ignored, the more relationships break-down and the greater resentment builds up.
Act ASAP!

'Isn't this what I've been paid to do for the past five years?'

This is a tricky question. Yes, it could be argued that senior managers who have been in office a long time are personally responsible for the condition of the organization. But let's remember two things:

- Corporate Denial is the result of a systemic breakdown, not the failure of one individual; and
- what we do now is far more important than what we have or haven't already done. With the best will in the world, none of us can change the past but we are all responsible for the future.

'We've only just reorganized'

Enough said.

'You don't want to rock the boat, it will damage your career'

Most abusive relationships are built on threats and intimidation. This is what keeps Corporate Denial alive and well. Those that succumb are condemning their organizations and themselves (whist they remain in the company) to a life of chronic Corporate Stress and underachievement.

Taking personal responsibility

At the end of the day at least one senior individual must stand up and lead the charge.

If that person controls the organization, they can immediately start trying to win the organization over to play an active role in the Truth and Reconciliation in Business project.

If not, they will have to convince the whole leadership team first and then engage the organization. Either way, there are some simple guidelines that will help.

Take immediate action

Time and truth wait for no man – act now.

Open the kimono

Open yourself up, be honest about your own strengths and weaknesses – show the real you.

Look after the eggs

Make sure that whilst you invest in Truth and Reconciliation in Business, you don't forget about the day-to-day reality of developing new business, serving customers and partnering suppliers.

Pick your first team

Go through the whole organization and pick a team to work with based on attitude and commitment, not seniority or position. Don't cross-infect your team by using uncommitted people.

This is not the time to start utilizing the people not wanted for anything else.

Think people and passion, not process

This is about attitude and honesty more than dotting i's and crossing t's.

Be inspiring

Think Churchill: 'We shall fight on the beaches', etc.

Seeking the truth

Truth and Reconciliation in Business is a solution unlike any other. It is a solution of the people, by the people for the people.

However it is inaugurated and whoever takes responsibility for starting the exercise it is the organization in all its constituent parts that must complete the process.

The key tool involved in Truth and Reconciliation in Business is Truth Map. I will discuss this more fully in the final section of the book, Relationship Mapping.

Truth Map is an audit process that involves representatives from across the whole organization reviewing the organization in a simple, structured way. The outcome is a red flag/green flag analysis of the organization's major functions and relationships. This becomes the sounding board from which to launch the rest of the Relationship Mapping process.

What is more important than the tool is the spirit in which the tool is used.

Truth and Reconciliation in Business is an invitation to creativity. It is an invitation to everybody within the organization to play their part in achieving what the hierarchy of the organization was either unable or unwilling to address on its own.

Individuals and groups from across every dimension of the organization – employees, stakeholders, even partners, suppliers and customers – can come together in the spirit of imagination, innovation and ingenuity to contribute in various ways and to search for possible solutions to previously insurmountable problems.

It is the active involvement and drive of individuals within an organization that makes Truth and Reconciliation in Business operational. They give it life and, by living it and going through it, a whole new organizational culture can flourish.

> **This is how ordinary is overcome and OK stops being OK!**

Acting consistently and decisively

Truth and Reconciliation in Business without consistent, decisive, action will rapidly turn into a nightmare.

Decisions and actions must be swift and if Relationship Mapping is to be engaged, it must be engaged fast and directly connected to the Truth and Reconciliation in Business exercise.

Communication will be at an absolute premium and there are several points that the exercise must deliver on.

Truth and Reconciliation in Business must:

- lift the lid on silence and Denial;
- give everyone within the organization the chance to have their grievances heard and their ideas listened to;
- use appropriate, direct language and avoid beating about the bush;
- view the organization as one entity, not separate entities with different expectations and responsibilities. Everybody involved must be equally responsible and accountable for all outcomes and there can be no splintering into different groups, as this will set the seed for different sub-cultures to grow back;
- accept the principle of mutual shared responsibility for any previous shortcomings of the organization;

- encourage the building of a new social network that straddles previous divides, and delivers ongoing dialogue and interaction across every dimension of the organization;
- determine what is negotiable and what is non-negotiable; and
- make clear recommendations for the future, start to define responsibilities, expectations and desired relationships, start the process of reform, and begin to define a working culture for the organization as a single entity.

Preventing repetition

The last and critically important stage in Truth and Reconciliation in Business is preventing repetition.

Life after Corporate Denial
Once an alcoholic ...

It is true that an individual is never entirely cured of an addiction, however long they stay clear of its clutches.

The same is true of organizations. Engaging in Truth and Reconciliation in Business is a great start for any organization looking to develop amazing relationships and enjoy amazing success, but it is only the start of the process.

Organizations must be able to maintain what they have started.

In the next and final section of the book I will introduce two concepts vital to preventing the return of Corporate Denial. These concepts are:

- Active Constitution; and
- Corporate Ritual.

Active Constitution is a way of formalizing an agreed working culture into a contract between all members of an organization and Corporate Ritual involves the ritualization of important corporate rites of passage.

Combined together they put flesh on the bones of Truth and Reconciliation in Business, creating a sense of belonging capable of uniting an organization and holding it together in the face of threat and distraction.

8.0 Relationship Mapping

How to build amazingly successful relationships

wjm

The road to Relationship Mapping

Relationship Mapping is the logical destination of everything I have come to understand about organizations. It is simple, direct and more about travelling the same road together than it is about process but also reflects the fact that detail, precision and clarity are vital when communicating anything to anyone.

It recognizes the importance of language and its power to unite an organization in an almost tribal way. It also understands that words can be distorted and become an enemy to cohesion when abused or neglected.

Relationship Mapping understands the logical sequences that need to be followed in order to establish an effective culture. It recognizes the need for a shared version of the truth before we can think about taking an organization forward.

But maybe the most fundamental lesson behind Relationship Mapping is about inclusiveness, honesty and mutual respect. Amazing success is based on amazing relationships and that means *all* relationships: relationships are two-way and without mutual respect, no relationship can ever be more than a transaction. Transactions do not bring loyalty and trust with them: they are intrinsically short-term and play no part in helping an organization to mature and evolve.

The elements of Relationship Mapping

Relationship Mapping is made up of several elements:

- Truth Map – arriving at a shared and accepted understanding of the challenges and opportunities facing an organization;
- Culture Map – helping people to work together effectively without wasted effort;
- Message Map – making it easy for people to hear you;
- Behaviour Map – helping people do the right things;
- Active Constitution – an accessible and empowering way to encapsulate, manage and share an organization's working culture; and
- Corporate Ritual – creating pride in the organization.

The history of Relationship Mapping

I have spent several years building and testing the component parts of Relationship Mapping, and as I learnt more about organizational relationships and their impact on overall organizational success, so the emphasis has changed from a series of component parts to a cohesive logical whole.

Truth Map and Culture Map have probably had the longest gestation period. I first started developing the principles for them about 16 years ago at BT when I was faced with the task of uniting 2500-plus separate sales, service and marketing staff into one cohesive group. We had to change the culture from 'civil service meets technology' to 'business consultant meets CEO', which I can tell you took quite some doing.

We had to take an organization focused almost exclusively internally, on age-old hierarchies, technology and product, and turn it inside out. Before we could create a customer-based culture we had to introduce the concept of customers!

When I joined the organization, customers were called subscribers and the concept of customer need was unheard of. Customers were faced with a stark choice: place their order and get it in three months, place it in a month's time and maybe get it in four months, or try to find an alternative supplier and face being out of communication with customers and suppliers alike.

The sales force was unlike anything I had previously encountered. They set their own targets, reported their own sales (actually orders received) and played as much golf as they could.

The only way to change the organization was to start from scratch. We almost put a wall around the sales and marketing functions and built a new organization inside that wall. This was not ideal, but the 'big BT' was still around 150,000 people: too big for us to influence and after all, we still had about 2500 people to play with as it was.

This was large-scale culture change and I borrowed heavily from the cultures I had experienced in retail buying offices such as Dixons and Debenhams, where customers were a way of life. We also learnt from the more established IT companies, where selling business advantage rather than technology was a bit more advanced.

For someone interested in people and relationships it was a bit like dying and going to heaven. I had 2500 people to experiment on and a massive culture change to effect.

Although I did not call them this at the time, we constructed the foundations of Truth Map and Culture Map over several years and we did it the hard way, using a process of trial and error. In the end it probably took about seven years of consistent effort to make a significant change to the culture.

This was one of the most exciting times of my life. I worked in a great team, with some great colleagues, and every day we did something different or faced a new challenge.

The most rewarding thing was seeing the organization grow before my eyes. Individuals would change from bureaucrats to consummate professionals and an organization with little character or purpose would grow in stature, confidence and effectiveness on a daily basis.

What was fascinating was the effect that the change in our division had on other parts of the organization. The customer focus spread right back into the organization and cross-functional relationships blossomed where previously there had been a relationship desert.

What we did may not have been enough to save the whole of BT from itself but it certainly proved an incredible learning ground for me and everyone else involved in the experience.

On leaving BT I fine-tuned my ideas at Ernst & Young for a time before recognizing that I needed to work in a much more fluid and creative environment if I was ever going to champion the development of effective relationships in organizations.

One major benefit of my time at Ernst & Young was meeting Tim Guy and David Birt. Tim and David worked together at Tim Guy Design, a communications company assisting Ernst & Young at the time. I soon discovered that they were approaching the same issues as me but from another point of view.

We hit it off virtually immediately and have been on a crusade to help clients communicate better and build better relationships ever since.

Charged with helping clients communicate, they were faced on an almost daily basis with a real conundrum. Their clients seemed to know what they wanted but could not say why. They also knew what they wanted their customers to think but could not explain clearly what would make them think it!

We recognized quickly that organizational purpose, relationships, internal and external communication, and behaviour all needed to be linked more strongly if these kinds of questions were to be answered.

Too many organizations were trying to communicate independently of an understanding of their core purpose and without direct reference to the relationships that the communication was designed to support.

This was the start of Message Mapping, which Tim and David have now refined into a fine art and which has proved invaluable to organizations time and time again.

The other elements of Relationship Mapping – Behaviour Map, Active Constitution and Corporate Ritual – have developed over the last few years as, working together with Annalese Banbury, my understanding of organizational dynamics and relationships has become more complete.

Truth Map: asking straight questions, being open to straight answers

Truth Map is an audit process designed to get to the bottom of an organization's challenges, opportunities and concerns.

It requires the involvement of a cross-section of individuals from right across the whole organization, as well as other relevant parties such as customers and suppliers. At its most simple level, it involves asking a lot of people a lot of questions – but that is only the beginning.

It is not what Truth Map is that makes it special but the reasons why it is being undertaken and the spirit in which it is carried out that are important.

I use Truth Map in two different situations, firstly as part of Truth and Reconciliation in Business, and secondly as the first stage of a standard Message Mapping exercise.

A Truth Map covers the same ground in either situation but covers it in different ways and for slightly different reasons.

- Used as part of a standard Message Mapping exercise (e.g. to assist a group of committed, enthusiastic individuals), the emphasis is on getting to the truth about future opportunities and challenges.
- Used as part of Truth and Reconciliation in Business, the emphasis is on getting to the truth of past conflicts, reconciling differences and healing resentments before an organization is even able to move on and address the future. In this type of situation, significant effort must be applied to bring the different parties to the table before dialogue and debate can even start to take place.

In both these situations the actual mechanics are much the same. Both situations require methodical, systematic but sympathetic questioning.

In the interests of objectivity, the presence of an independent adjudicator can be highly beneficial or even essential.

Truth Map allows everyone to be heard, it airs people's grievances and, when done well, even the most hardened objectors can move from being on the outside peeing in, to being on the inside peeing out!

I conducted a Truth Map for a state secondary school that was looking to achieve specialist engineering college status. At the start of the exercise the school was riddled with dissent and dissatisfaction. Feelings were running high about many issues, not least the whole concept of specialist schools, with words such as 'obscene' and 'disgusting' banded about. Large sections of the school saw no value in the engineering specialism and departments such as modern languages, RE, drama, etc. saw it as a direct threat to their funding.

Parents and pupils were unclear as to the benefits of the change and an old-fashioned 19th-century view of engineering was at the forefront of people's minds.

By the time the exercise was complete, 'engineering' had been converted into 'discovery', links had been established with leading-edge hi-tech commercial organizations, the pupils were enthusiastic and a couple of the teaching staff who previously could only have been described as resistance fighters became leading forces in the whole drive towards becoming a specialist engineering college.

Failure to properly address the issues raised during this exercise would not only have caused the school to miss out on exciting new opportunities but could have caused it to split it in two and damaged every aspect of the school's spirit and performance.

That is how important Truth Map can be; it doesn't deliver just marginal advantage, it can change the whole future of an organization!

The mechanics of Truth Map

1 Constructing the audit

Truth Map investigates every aspect of an organization's performance that can impact on the overall effectiveness of its relationships. Although there is no single way of configuring a Truth Map, I usually use the following parameters to conduct the audit.

Audience groups:

- leadership team;
- management group;
- employees;
- market place – customers and suppliers;
- shareholders and other stakeholders; and
- community and environment.

Performance parameters:

- purpose and direction;
- leadership and communication;
- performance and innovation;
- teamwork and culture;
- products and services;
- customer service, sales and client management;
- identity, look and feel; and
- information and knowledge.

As a guide I have provided in Appendix 3 an idea of the types of questions I ask under each of these parameters. These questions are only intended as a starter for ten – the level of detail required to conduct a real Truth Map is far greater than this – but they will provide guidance as to where to start.

2 Asking the questions

Knowing the right questions to ask is a start but the way an audit is conducted is what determines the eventual outcome of the exercise.

I generally conduct interviews on a one-to-one basis or, if people prefer, in small groups.

People need to know that their position will not be compromised in anyway because I need a level of candour that is unusual in business situations. I have to break through the usual platitudes that people come out with at the start of an interview, which is not always easy. I have to establish a bond of trust with the person I am talking to and the whole interview usually lasts no longer than an hour, so I have to work fast.

Remember that these interviews are conducted with every type of person, from aggressive and defensive directors to rather intimidated junior employees. Everyone must be made to feel comfortable, both with me and with the whole process.

Conducting these interviews is an intense and draining experience. I usually conduct several one after another through the course of the day and at the end of the day feel fairly drained and ready for a long cool beer.

But they can also be vastly rewarding when individuals start to open up. It is sometimes actually quite moving and humbling seeing first-hand the passion that some employees feel for their company.

This is when I enjoy my job most, when I can help an organization harness the raw and untapped passion contained within; it is an amazing experience to be part of. Working in a great organization is a privilege and being able to help an organization of this nature is an even greater privilege.

The next stage of the challenge is to take the sparks of interest and excitement that have been lit and turn them into a roaring furnace.

3 Creating a first impression

Once the questions have been asked I construct an outline Truth Map (see Figure 8.1), taking audience groups and performance parameters as the two co-ordinates and completing a simple traffic light analysis.

Although only top-level, this still provides a useful first-glance indication of the state of the organization.

4 Telling stories

Once the straight questions have been asked and a draft Truth Map created, the second critical stage of Truth Map begins; turning plain facts into an organizational parable.

People find direct criticism hard to swallow however nicely it is put and however much they might be seeking to deal with things honestly.

Over the years I have discovered that the trick to making the truth palatable is to tell a story that everyone can hear and relate to without feeling directly threatened.

- I rarely write reports for people, choosing instead to create parables that I can deliver as a show or performance to those that were involved in stage one of the exercise.

	Leadership team	Management group	Employees	Market place – customers and suppliers	Shareholders and other stakeholders	Community and environment
Purpose and direction	Grey	Grey	Black	Black	Black	Black
Leadership and communication	Grey	White	White	White	White	Black
Performance and innovation	White	White	White	White	Grey	Grey
Teamwork and culture	Grey	White	Black	Black	Black	Grey
Products and services	White	White	White	Grey	White	Grey
Customer service, sales and client management	Black	Grey	White	Grey	White	Grey
Identity, look and feel	White	White	White	White	White	Grey
Information and knowledge	Grey	White	White	White	Grey	White

Figure 8.1 Outline Truth Map

White: good relationships. Grey: improvements needed. Black: signs of Denial

- I use my passion, humour and honesty to make people sit up and listen. I tell hard truths but in a way that I hope makes people want to shout 'let's do something about it!', not 'let's do something about him!'
- I avoid direct blame and try to use good communication and theatre to inspire people to act.
- I never pull my punches but I always try to avoid making anyone feel small or vulnerable.

This stage of Truth Map is crucial because everyone must feel that their views, however downbeat or critical, have been heard and not swept under the carpet, and at the same time you must create hope and excitement about a better, united future.

You must support the leadership team but also empower the whole organization; balance is critical.

Once Truth Map has been completed, the really big question raises its head: 'what's next?'

This is where insight must rapidly be turned into action before enthusiasm turns into pessimism.

> **The worst thing in the world for an organization's health is to conduct a Truth Map and then do nothing about it.**

Which leads on to Culture Map.

Culture Map: proactive culture management

Culture Map turns accidents into design and business associates into a team.

Culture Map is not just a process; it represents the belief that being the best we can be is important, that being proud of what we do at work matters. It is a kick in the teeth for any cynics who think that people and relationships don't matter.

It would be easy to be disheartened by the cynics and start questioning our beliefs. *What is so wrong with doing what we can get away with? So what if we duck our responsibilities and settle for an easy and profitable life?*

The answer to these questions comes down to personal conscience and personal choice. I would rather sell doughnuts on a beach in France than sell my life and soul to a corporation that I can't believe in, and I know from many separate experiences that I am not unique in this.

But confronting Denial and Culture Map won't be for everyone. As I always say, only read this book if ordinary is no longer OK!

Culture Map is dedicated to those of us that share this belief!

Culture Map explained

Culture Map turns random culture generation into a managed process, producing cultures capable of uniting organizations around a common purpose and creating the foundation of sound, consistent, effective relationships that put organizations on track to achieve their short-term goals and long-term aspirations.

Before an organization can work as a team it must be clear about what it wants, how it intends to get it and why it matters. This is the ground that many organizations try and cover using vision and mission statements and where so many of them fall at the first fence.

There are several fundamental reasons why so many of these 'statements' consistently fail to achieve what, in many cases, are creditable goals.

- They are often written in poorly defined and intimidating language – employees often don't understand them and view them as remote and irrelevant to their world.
- Once they are written down, that's it – no review process or code of conduct is put in place to tell people how the vision and mission statements should be used or what they are actually for.

This is why vision and mission have acquired, albeit unfairly, an appalling reputation. They have been implemented so badly in organizations across the country that people have come to regard the statements themselves as the problem, not the fact that they have been used badly.

I have abandoned the terms 'vision' and 'mission' and created Culture Map as a solution complete with user guide. It is far removed from the static, disconnected and discredited collection of words that vision and mission statements have unfortunately become.

Implementing Culture Map

Culture Map is a 52-weeks-a-year experience that should ultimately become a living part of an organization. It is not a framed set of words to be dusted down every so often and brought out for annual reports, corporate inspections or stuck, bizarrely and very much out of context, in front of client pitches.

Culture Map needs to be based on detailed and thorough self-examination enriched by relevant external perspectives brought about by exercises such as Truth Map.

Culture Map is about doing basic, logical things extremely well and doing them in a way that includes everyone and links every part of the organization. That means including those interested parties outside the core headcount as well as those on the payroll.

It is not clever or complicated and it is certainly not rocket science but it is much needed because too many organizations are still getting things horribly wrong.

> **The spirit in which Culture Map is entered into, the way it is conducted and the way the process is communicated are what lead Culture Map to succeed or fail.**

Culture Maps must be:

- led by the whole leadership team and inclusive of the whole organization;
- developed in conjunction with shareholders and partners;
- an interactive and iterative experience, encouraging responsible involvement and dialogue;
- a transparent and integral process;
- uncluttered, unambiguous, direct and central to business decision-making;
- able to genuinely differentiate the organization from competitors;
- able to deliver control through effective delegation;
- relevant and meaningful to everyone in the organization, articulating appropriate corporate values;
- used as the guideline for how to ensure the organization's values form the basis of corporate identity, brand, market messages, team behaviours, customer service and all organizational relationships; and
- inspirational and exciting.

Culture Map consists of five stages; defining purpose, laying the foundation of key relationships, buying in the organization, articulating corporate values and culture building.

1 Purpose definition

This section is purely designed to provide context to the following sections. It is not an end in itself and should be kept short, sweet and to the point.

- **Core purpose:** Culture Maps are task-related and must state what the organization is trying to achieve, how success is going to be defined and how it will be measured. This should not be long-winded and complicated but provide a very precise description which clearly differentiates the organization from all other competitors, failure to do this will result in a weak Culture Map.
- **Primary goals:** what are the most important things the organization must achieve? These must include a mixture of short-, medium- and long-term goals. Key goals should be limited to a workable number and be prioritized and weighted in importance.
- **Key measures:** every goal must be measurable and each measure must have targets and timescales.
- **Review process:** an open review process must be identified from the outset. This must allow for a thorough and inclusive review, and should be multi-directional rather than purely cascade. Review must cover performance against purpose and goals, but most importantly in the context of Culture Map it must feature a review of both corporate and individual behaviour and relationships against stated intentions.

Part one of Culture Map is designed as a way of grounding desired culture in the goals of the business. Far too often in my experience business objectives and working culture are developed in isolation with disastrous implications for all concerned – including the customers.

2 Defining key relationships

This is the vital ingredient in Culture Map.

An effective Culture Map determines an organization's key relationships through clearly laid-out priorities and principles.

This includes relationships between the organization and:

- its products
- its market place

- its investors
- its customers
- its leadership team
- its employees
- its partners
- its suppliers
- the government and regulation
- the local areas in which it operates
- the environment
- society generally.

A full description of each of these relationships is required. Relationship descriptions must be detailed as this information will be the basis for clarifying appropriate values, decision-making criteria, behaviour and organizational structure. The organization needs these relationships in order to survive and prosper, so they have to be described correctly and honestly. All assertions must be linked back to corporate purpose and goals, and supported by examples, evidence, proof and demonstration.

These relationships have to be described in such a way that they become tangible and meaningful to everyone. The process must also be transparent, with everybody involved throughout the whole process.

Working these relationship descriptions up to a level that they are meaningful will not be easy. You will have to make tough choices and face some hard facts. You will have to be honest and upfront with people whilst still working to maintain enthusiasm and momentum.

The relationships need to be prioritized: when everything is of equal importance the result is chaos. Different individuals end up using their own judgement and organizational splits are born. Ignoring hard facts does not make them go away and hiding things under the carpet only results in people tripping over.

Try ranking the above relationships from one to twelve in order of importance; it can be a revealing exercise. This is one of the things I do in organizational boardrooms: I go through these relationships with each board member individually, asking them to prioritize them and then explain their reasons and the implications they think their choice would have on the organization. I encourage them to be honest about their view of the current state of these relationships and about ideas to move the organization forward.

Then comes the tricky part; bringing them together to discuss it!

I draw heavily on the experiences of Truth and Reconciliation at a national level in shaping my approach to creating organizational harmony overall, but when I am in the boardroom arena I revert to lessons learnt from relationship guidance.

Anyone who has been through relationship counselling or knows someone that has will know how hard the process can be and that is usually with just two people (at least in the room if not in the relationship).

When you are faced with not two but six to ten people all holding passionate beliefs, strong vested interests and histories laced with hurt, resentment and pride, the scene is set for a fair old showdown.

I have come to rely heavily on straightforward honesty, humour, storytelling, silence, empathy and fair-handedness, and, when need be, calling a spade a spade.

They say never bluff a bluffer and calling people's bluff has become an occupational hazard for me, but as an organizational coach and troubleshooter I have also had to learn what I can and can't do.

I cannot solve people's problems; I can only help them solve their own problems.

I must respect individual views that I don't agree with.

I am also only allowed to work with teams while I retain the trust and respect of the *whole* team. This involves constantly walking a tightrope between being cruel to be kind, saying what I believe to be true and letting people progress at a pace that is right for them and in a direction that they are all comfortable with.

I have to deal with issues of personal style and integrity, helping directors to be honest about issues that they may never have had to openly discuss before.

This is a major step for all concerned and can be heart-rending stuff.

I have come to realise that passions run just at high at work as they do at home; the difference is that the awareness of the role relationships play at work is much lower than it is in personal situations.

In the overwhelmingly macho world of boardrooms, where women can be as macho as men, openness – and, dare I say it, expressing genuine feelings – is currently an anathema.

'So what?' you might say. 'That's just the way it is, has always been and always will be.'

Wrong ...

> **Better relationships at all levels within business make more money and deliver longer, more soundly based success, and the tone for business relationships is set in the boardroom.**

To understand the scale of the change that is needed, think about relationships between men and women today and compare them with just 40 years ago in the 1960s – there has been a revolution.

I believe that a change in attitudes to relationships at work and to the way that relationships are thought about and conducted will change organizations just as radically as society generally has already changed.

> **Just as Ikea challenges us to 'chuck out the chintz', let's stop accepting ordinary as OK and go for it.**

For more detail on the principles of effective relationships, see Appendix 2.

3 Opening up to the whole organization

Sorting out the leadership team is only step one. Relationship definitions must be tested and further developed throughout the organization.

Sharing the leadership team's view on relationship priorities with employees and other parties is always going to be a robust but hopefully fruitful experience.

It is impossible to get people to buy into this type of work if they are excluded from the process and the solutions will never be as workable without extended involvement.

I am often pleasantly surprised by the reaction received from the organization at large: vested interests are less extreme and, surprisingly, people can be less cynical. There is often a pool of positive energy lying under a crust of disillusioned middle management that can put leaders to shame.

The success of Culture Map is all in the implementation. I have too often seen defeat grasped out of the jaws of victory due to poor communication and implementation to ever assume anything when it comes to organizational change.

> **The ability of sane people to do nine fantastic things
> and then cap it off with one ill-considered shortcut
> still has the power to surprise me.**

4 Corporate values

Values come in for a bad press alongside vision and mission, and I am one of the first to criticize the way that some organizations play around with them.

But as with vision and mission, the problems lie not with the values themselves but with those responsible for them.

The greatest mistake with corporate values is hanging them in thin air with nothing above and below them:

- they are unrelated to a realistic analysis of the overall organizational purpose, goals and the relationships they are designed to deliver;
- they are not made meaningful and relevant in the context of day-to-day situations and required behaviours; and
- they are poorly shared with the organization.

> **In short, no-one ever knows where values come from,
> what they mean or what to do with them!**

Culture Map overcomes these shortcomings by building values out of desired relationships and converting them into everyday usage through Behaviour Map and Message Map.

Creating values

Take each relationship in turn and identify half a dozen values specifically related to each relationship.

These values can be defined far more accurately because they can now be viewed in a situational context and this means several things:

- the exact meaning of each value can be defined in a level of detail that makes them meaningful but does not create confusion;

- a single value can mean two different things when related to two different relationships but it is not confusing if the detail is supplied;
- the different priorities of different parts of the organization can be equally and fairly reflected;
- not all values need be equally relevant to everyone, only to those who are involved with the appropriate relationship; and
- each individual within the organization can have their own separately prioritized package of values based on the relationships they are required to conduct; however, there should be no direct contradictions between the values of one part of an organization and any other part.

5 Developing and sharing culture

It is essential for any agreed Culture Map to be clearly documented so that everyone in the organization can fully understand it and actively use it as a yardstick for decision-making and relationship-building.

Documentation should include guidelines as to how performance will be reviewed, bearing in mind that, in effect, it becomes a mutually binding contract between the organization, its leaders and all its employees.

Everyone must expect to be held accountable for their personal behaviour and the way they interpret corporate values in making decisions on behalf of the organization.

At the end of this chapter I will discuss Active Constitutions and Corporate Ritual, which hold the key to the effective communication and sharing of Culture Map.

Remember:

> **The greater the precision, candour, excitement and rigour with which an organization expresses its desired Culture Map, the greater the integrity with which it can behave. No organization can act with integrity outside of its chosen culture.**

Message Map

Message Map is one of the ways that we make sure Culture Map works at the coalface.

Originally developed by David Birt and Tim Guy, Message Map has helped numerous organizations save money, improve their internal and external communication, and is often pivotal in instructing the whole branding and identity process.

We are now using it to cascade a logical process from organizational goals all the way down to choosing the appropriate media to communicate the right messages to the right audiences.

There have been a number of occasions where we have had to embark on a Message Map exercise prematurely within the Relationship Mapping cycle, purely because of an organization's refusal to believe that they were unable to describe with the required degree of clarity and consensus what they were looking to achieve and how this fitted with overall organizational goals.

Only when these clients have tried and failed to provide the relevant answers with the crispness and level of agreement required have they believed that there must be bigger issues to be sorted before they can communicate effectively.

When it comes to external relationships, some organizations prefer to 'communicate and be damned' than put the work in first to get the whole organization going in the same direction. This is why some companies end up wasting millions on ill-conceived rebranding, advertising, web sites and marketing ventures.

Taking some executives to a communications or advertising agency is a bit like taking a child to a candy store or a toy shop. Common sense and reason go out of the window and the whole glitz and glamour of the situation seems to turn even the most normal and rational of heads. I have realized that even finance directors and heads of engineering have a propensity to secretly fancy themselves as marketing guys and can be swayed into supporting actions that they would never normally agree to.

By conducting a Message Map we can sometimes lift the red mist and stop organizations wasting huge amounts of money on stuff that can actually undermine and damage their customer relationships rather than advance their interests.

So how does each step of Message Map work?

1   **Organizational goals:** ensure that communication objectives relate back directly to organizational goals.

2   **Organizational values:** consider the relevance of corporate values to proposed communication and consider the impact that communication may have on internal and external perception of the organization's values.

3   **Key audiences:** prioritize the target audiences and explain why they are important.

4   **Desired actions:** list the actions you want each audience to take.

5   **Decision-making criteria:** list the decision-making criteria of each audience for each action.

6   **Customer perceptions:** Identify current, desired and competitive perceptions against each of the decision-making criteria.

7   **Messages:** draft messages against perception triggers.

8   **Proof, demonstration and evidence:** find evidence to support each message.

9   **Media:** identify the right media for each message to each audience and calculate the degree of message resistance in each case so that an appropriate campaign can be constructed.

Relationships and communication

It has become clear that the twin concepts of relationships and communication run through each other like thread through a needle. For one to succeed they must both succeed: over-focusing on one at the expense of the other causes waste and pain.

Organizations however are currently more used to investing in market communication than in building effective relationships. Communication is more tangible than the relationships that underlie it and budgets are usually already set aside for communication but not for relationships, which are only considered to be important when they are going pear-shaped.

The challenge facing organizations is to be far more imaginative in their attitude to relationships and communication, and to see them properly for what they are: two ends of the same thing.

Relationships and communication both need constant, ongoing development and maintenance rather than the stop-go 'feast and famine' approach in vogue today.

Message Map works – it has a proven track record – but it works best when an organization is clear about the way it wants its overall purpose, key goals, culture, relationships, communication and team behaviour to work together.

Which brings me on to the last Map in the series: Behaviour Map.

Behaviour Map

Behaviour Map is similar to Message Map but is used to determine team behaviour rather than market messages.

Behaviour Map is an effective way of getting over one of the greatest objections to organizational values: that it is hard to make them relevant to individual situations. The primary purpose of Behaviour Map is to make it easy for each individual to convert organizational values into clear, actionable behaviours.

The impact that Behaviour Map can have on an organization committed to living by a single culture is immense, but it works better as part of an overall culture plan than acted out in isolation.

The key elements of Behaviour Map are:

1 Key relationships and values

Behaviour Map refers back to the relationships that were defined within Culture Map and builds on the values that were identified to support each key relationship.

2 Organizational structure

Having established the key relationships and values of an organization it is important to make sure that the organization is structured in such a way that these relationships can be enhanced and not obstructed, obscured or confused.

Is the current structure a legacy of the past and is it helping or hindering tight customer focus?

Structure is a mandatory requirement if an organization is to hold together and keep control, but by the same token it can also be a great inhibitor and can greatly hinder effectiveness and performance.

The key is to find the least damaging structure that delivers the greatest benefit and often this requires help from an external source not influenced by vested interests. The desire to build empires still lurks just below the surface in many organizations.

There is unlikely to be a perfect solution, but one thing is for sure: organizations built around their key relationships rather than by function will undoubtedly fare better because they are more likely to be driven by market issues than management agendas.

3 Required skills

Once we have checked an organization's structure against key relationships, the organization must ensure that it has the right skills in the right places.

Key skills need to be identified by department.

4 Desired behaviours

Defining the way we want people to behave is the next step. How do we want people to use their skills to deliver the relationships that need to be maintained?

How can the organization's values be turned into understandable and auditable behaviours?

This is a big step forward for many organizations and provides what has long been a missing link in managing corporate reputation and delivering consistent customer service.

The approach described here can be adapted to fit every type of role, not just customer-facing functions. It is as relevant to board directors as it is to sales assistants.

5 Motivations

Having defined desired behaviours, we can begin to motivate people to do the right things.

Organizations need to understand that people are motivated by different things and that they need to link performance and behaviour with what will inspire particular individuals.

This means putting as much time into understanding our staff as understanding what we want them to achieve.

It also means taking a more flexible approach to individual reward and recognition. Many organizations shy away from this type of idea because they think it is too much trouble to bother with, but in so doing, end up spending far more to get significantly less.

6 Incentives, remuneration, reward and recognition

A great deal of money is wasted by organizations who implement ineffective and occasionally damaging 'reward and recognition' policies. Many bonus schemes are irrelevant to how people perform and some even reward behaviour that is at odds to the organizational goals!

The cost of conducting a Behaviour Map exercise can often be justified by the financial saving of restructuring benefits alone!

Organizations must ensure that they are rewarding the right things and that rewarding them makes a difference.

Taking out the arbitrary elements in reward and recognition can bring significant savings and major benefits in its own right.

7 Demonstration

Demonstration is all about being seen to do what you want others to do. As every message requires proof, so every desired behaviour requires demonstration.

You cannot in any circumstance ask your team to behave in a way that you do not adhere to yourself.

Behaviour Map will only work if standards of expectation are applicable to every area and level within the organization.

Can you back up your desired behaviours?

- Who are the organizational role models?
- Are there role models of both sexes for people to relate to?
- Are there role models in every part of the organization?

- Do any senior managers devalue the process by their behaviour?
- Is desired behaviour reflected in and supported by the organization's policies and standard practice?
- Are desired behaviours and organizational messages aligned?

Without both personal and organizational demonstration at every level, it is much harder to control behaviour. Truly great managers do this instinctively and great relationships are built on it; think about any strong relationships you know of between parents and children. Great parents act as role models to their children – great relationships can never be born out of a 'do as I say, not as I do' mentality.

8 Communication

In retail it is 'location, location, location'; in relationships and behaviour change it is 'communication, communication, communication'. Nothing much can be achieved without a whole-hearted commitment to the highest levels of internal communication.

9 Feedback and review

Issuing orders might be fine in the army but in most organizations today it will not work well at all. A cornerstone of any Behaviour Map is consensus and an integral part of achieving consensus is transparent 360-degree feedback.

Active Constitution and Corporate Ritual

> 'The great and poignant paradox of our lives was that we had fought with all our passion to create a boring society.
>
> 'Could it be that once we had achieved our ideals, we could no longer live for them? I felt miserably neutered by the normality for which we had fought.'
>
> The Soft Vengeance of a Freedom Fighter, Albie Sachs, 2000

Fighting to achieve a goal and then living life after the initial goals have been achieved are two very different things.

Maintaining the life and spirit of an organization so that ordinary never becomes OK is as great a challenge as setting up an organization properly in the first place.

Because of this I have been developing Active Constitution and Corporate Ritual. Both of these are used to inject the results of Relationship Mapping into the lifeblood of an organization.

Active Constitution makes things real; Corporate Ritual makes them exciting.

Active Constitution

Nothing truly amazing in organizational terms can be achieved overnight. Consistency is important to building the trust needed to deliver amazing success.

To make an organization consistent it must be bigger than any one individual, in the way a football club has to be more important than any individual player.

This is where Active Constitution comes in.

Active Constitution is a way of capturing all the results of Relationship Mapping in a way that is accessible to the whole organization. It is the English Magna Carta and the US Constitution and Bill of Rights all rolled into one and applied to an organization.

Active Constitution forms a contract between the organization and all of its employees. It sets out what is expected of each individual and in return what can be expected of the organization.

It can take whatever physical form and tone is appropriate to the organization and can be as formal or informal as the culture of the organization dictates.

It is the pre-nuptial agreement of organizations!

It is designed to set out the organization's DNA, the genetic code that runs through everything an organization does. It connects its strategy to its brand and links leadership and communication.

It should be capable of uniting everybody from finance to marketing and position the CEO fairly and squarely as brand champion.

An Active Constitution needs to have some meat in it!

It should be:

- meaningful – work for each individual;
- exciting – motivate people to share the ideals;
- accessible – create an open, fair and understood organization; and
- tangible – provide an effective base for delegation and decision-making.

It must be used every day, not stored in a cupboard or on a shelf: Active Constitutions are a living, vibrant thing, not a static, dead document.

It should define how the organization and its leaders can be expected to behave and what responsibilities each party has to each other, and can form the foundation of corporate and social responsibility.

Active Constitutions work because they form a barrier against Denial and provide a yardstick against which everyone's behaviour, including that of the CEO and chairman, can be measured. No-one is beyond being held to account under the terms of the organization's Active Constitution.

**Active Constitution creates a trust-based,
not power-based, culture.**

Corporate Ritual

Corporate Ritual is a lost art in many organizations. It harks back to the days of guilds and clubs, where loyalty and a sense of belonging were important

Corporate Ritual is the icing on the Relationship Mapping cake. It is every birthday party and personal celebration translated into an organizational context.

It is about fun, it is about bonding and it is about rites of passage.

Corporate Ritual is what holds an organization together. It is what some small organizations are naturally masterful at but what large organizations fail to even try to achieve.

We are not just talking about getting drunk at Christmas parties and fumbling in broom cupboards. We are talking about marking significant events in the life of the organization and in the lives of employees with the ceremony and respect they deserve.

In the old days, people were given a watch or a clock to signify 25 or 30 years' service to the same organization. Bizarre as it might now seem viewed from a 21st-century perspective, for many people these were their most prized possessions.

Time has moved on and Corporate Ritual must now mean different things, but the principles are the same.

Corporate Ritual means marking people's arrival in an organization not just in terms of an effective induction process but through a welcoming ceremony.

It means recognizing all major achievements and marking the contribution of those involved in the success. It is about making the time to recognize and appreciate the personal dedication and sacrifice of individuals, and the significant successes and endeavours of the organization as a whole.

It is a return to the importance of organizational pride.

Corporate Ritual relies on:

- the art of theatre;
- ceremony;
- generating a sense of belonging and pride;
- good design;
- honest communication; and
- a shared recognition of the importance of human values and contribution.

Corporate Ritual is not frivolous or lightweight; it has beliefs and standards, and expects them to be adhered to.

It is the antipathy of the cynical, world-weary view common to organizations in Denial. It abhors running things by the lowest common denominator and the aspiration to be adequate.

As part of Relationship Mapping and in the spirit of the other ideas contained in this book, Corporate Ritual takes ideas more commonly associated with personal relationships and family values and applies them to organizations.

> **Corporate Ritual is the spirit of relationships in action:**
> **it does not believe in ordinary and is not embarrassed**
> **to celebrate personal or collective success.**

Corporate Denial in perspective

In the course of this book I have explored the very heart of what makes organizations succeed. I have demonstrated that you don't have to be an amazing organization to succeed to a point and that many organizations never will be amazing. And good luck to all of them!

The ideas in this book are born out of years of experience, excitement and frustration, and can be used in many ways. Even taking tiny elements of the book and applying them piecemeal, one bit at a time, can make a difference – and if 20 years has taught me anything it is that anyone can create the first splash and begin to change things, however large the pond and however small the ripple!

No matter how deeply an organization may be suffering Denial, just one person beginning to do the right things can change the experience of clients, colleagues and stakeholders of that organization.

But if *Corporate Denial* can be used to help organizations bit by bit when applied in a small way, then it is to those who embrace it wholeheartedly and really set about making a change to whom I dedicate this book.

We are all free individuals rather than victims and we all have more choices than ever. Help your organization to be the best it can be, be brave, embrace relationships and never accept ordinary as OK.

APPENDIX

1

What Culture?

Stereotypical working cultures: the good, the bad and the OK

wjm

What Culture?

How many different working cultures are there? I'm not sure whether there are an infinite number but I know that there are a lot! In fact there are probably as many different working cultures as there are organizations, but it is certainly still possible to identify some main stereotypes.

My colleagues and I have come up with a list of 12 different culture types that seem to cover the most obvious examples.

To help you identify what type of culture already exists in your organization and to aid you when considering the most appropriate culture to move your organization forward, I have conducted a working culture road test!

YOU ARE CORDIALLY INVITED TO

The *What Culture?* Culture of the Year Awards

For anyone in the market for a new working culture, this is a must-read article. We have lined up the world's leading work cultures for your benefit and delectation, and our experts have taken each culture for a spin over every conceivable organizational terrain so that you, the punter, can choose the right one!

THE CONTENDERS

We have split the working cultures into six categories based on which part of the organizational world is most likely to be the key relationship focus, prime advocate and beneficiary of the culture ...

Organization-centric: results culture, brand culture, institutional culture, exploitation culture.
Leader-centric: performance culture.
Employee-centric: recognition culture, rights culture, independence culture.
Customer-centric: service culture.
Investor-centric: profit culture.
Community-centric: partnership culture, philanthropy culture.

Results culture: organization-centric

The results culture puts a heavy emphasis on pragmatism and is most commonly found in start-up Primitive Organizations. Under the results culture overall team performance is seen as paramount and the end is seen to justify the means.

There is a heavy expectation on all individuals to buy into and support the goals of the organization, and to be self-motivated as a result. Support can be based either on a belief in the principles of the business or the prospects of the business: all that is required is unstinting support. Failure to deliver this is likely to lead rapidly to expulsion of an individual from the group.

There is something of the fanatic about the results culture and it is likely to be an extremely intense experience that can be very rewarding or very draining.

Strengths
No other culture can rival this one for getting the job done. This is the pick-up truck of the culture world, beloved by builders and revolutionaries the world over: no-frills but unstoppable and starts every time. Not necessarily beautiful, but it does more than you can expect of it.

Weaknesses
The only weakness of this culture is that it takes it out

> "... an extremely tense experience that can be very rewarding or very draining ..."

of you in the long run: you'll know you have been on a long, dusty, bumpy ride.

Overall verdict ★★★★
If this was more sustainable it would probably be the ideal culture. One of the few to countenance sacrifice of any kind, it has a tendency to almost take things too far.

This is without doubt one of the most cost-effective cultures, but sooner or later everyone becomes worn out, nerves become frayed and, if the organization neglects to take time out, relationships start to go wrong.

As an organization grows it needs to develop structure to do the things that shared enthusiasm achieves naturally.

Communication particularly starts to suffer with size, and the need to communicate seems to grow almost exponentially with the addition of new people if relationships are to retain any consistency.

There isn't a better way to start an organization than by adopting the results culture – but the crucial issue is knowing when to move on.

Timing and style will be everything, and those that rely on the results culture too long will suffer relationship stress as a result.

Brand culture: organization-centric

The brand culture is the natural organizational successor to the Personality Ethic as described by Stephen Covey: it sees success as a function of personality and public image. It concentrates on skills and techniques, and uses power base strategies to dominate others, alternating between coercion, intimidation, manipulation and influence to get what is required.

Relationships are very much a means to an end under the brand culture and whether aimed at competitors, employees, customers or shareholders, domination is key. The superficial takes on excessive importance and issues such as employee satisfaction and customer care are doomed to struggle up the priority list.

The brand culture is particularly prevalent in fast-growth markets such as the mobile phone market of recent years, where attracting new customers was more important than minimizing churn on existing ones.

Strengths

If you want a sporty, good-looking culture, this is the one for you. With the fastest 0–60 of any of the contenders, we were well impressed. This is also the culture to impress your friends with: highly versatile, whatever they are looking for the brand culture has the solution.

Well-presented, it comes in an amazing variety of colours and is beautifully packaged as well. The brand culture can make the most of very little and has the added benefit of being very fast to set up. No awkward instruction manuals with this one: just get in and off you go.

Not necessarily one for the faint-hearted, you can't run one of these on the cheap. This is a culture that demands to be out and about, and expects to be seen at all the coolest venues.

This culture will definitely provide you with a thrill around every corner, but expect a short attention span and make sure you are never short of a new idea to keep it entertained at all times.

Weaknesses

Despite its massive showroom appeal, the brand culture has one major drawback: build quality! Don't be surprised when your front end goes one way and your back end is all over the place. Although you can expect to turn quite a few heads when it arrives, be prepared for a few laughs on the way home when your friends pass you broken down on the hard shoulder.

As well as the poor build quality, expect massive depreciation and high running costs. This culture flatters to deceive: expect to pay heavily for those first few months when you were the envy of all your friends.

Overall verdict ★★★

This culture is loved by advertising managers and people obsessed with the latest idea. Despite that, this is a culture with some merit. The inventor of go-faster stripes, fluffy dice and leg warmers, it undoubtedly still has a role to play.

Many of the outstanding features are indeed brilliant and it can generate an adrenalin rush unlike any other culture; but as the saying goes, 'caveat emptor' – or 'buyer beware'!

It is about glitz and glamour and putting on a good show, and speed and change are its mantra. The real virtues at the heart of its appeal are without question valuable in fostering creativity, innovation and a sense of urgency and excitement amongst everybody that they touch. But try and find a way to harness the benefits without the fundamental relationship flaws.

When I left university I went to work in retail buying for retailers such as House of Fraser, Top Man, Dorothy Perkins and so on, which was a real eye opener. When you work in the buying department of a major retailer you very rapidly learn about the strengths of a strong, cohesive brand.

Sitting in the middle of Dorothy Perkins' buying office – with the lingerie department on one side and dresses on the other – as part of a team made up of seven women and me made me grow up fast. Everything that was said and done during the course of a day was focused on our target market of young women. There were clothes everywhere and if you did not eat, sleep and drink ladies' fashion, you were doomed.

When I moved to Top Man, the buying office was totally different, not in what it did but in the style it did it. A laddish youthfulness was present even down to what people wore, what they read and ultimately how they thought.

Only by taking on the brand and becoming immersed in their customers' world can any large buying office turn out a single co-ordinated look when the merchandize hits the store.

This is the power of a strong brand culture at its best, immersing all those involved in the market place.

The institutional culture: organization-centric

This is the culture of choice for monopolies, institutions, protected markets and some government bodies.

Self-importance and a God-given right to exist feature strongly. The primary beneficiaries are always those within the organization and the victims are usually customers.

Strengths
In automotive terms the institutional culture is a cross between a Hummer and a Rover, the sort of car it is better to be driving than stuck behind on a winding road.

This is the perfect culture if you think the world owes you a living.

Weaknesses
If the institutional culture was a motorist, it would drive along in the middle lane of an empty motorway at 60mph and stare at you in an annoyed way when you overtake.

The institutional culture has so many weaknesses it is hard to know where to start. This is a culture that makes the old Austin Allegro seem racy.

> "... this is a culture that makes the old Austin Allegro seem racy ..."

Overall verdict ★★
Surely no-one who uses this culture can seriously believe that they are doing the right thing but I would estimate that it is still one of the most widely used.

Both those that enjoy taking advantage and those so steeped in Corporate Denial that they no longer recognize that they are taking advantage love this culture. This is the perfect culture for those that love playing games and succeed by studying the rules at length, then mastering the art of turning rules to their own advantage. Relationships are just another game to be played to maximum advantage and from lawyers through local authority officials to the depths of academia, there are thousands of people making very comfortable livings in this way.

The greatest strength of this culture is its ability to unify; I have never experienced any other culture that can so completely take over an organization. From the receptionist to the CEO, this culture can insure that everyone learns to put the organization's interests first.

The exploitation culture: organization-centric

The basic premise that underlies this culture is that of infinite supply: that there will always be an infinite supply of new ideas, new products, new employees, new customers and new shareholders to be exploited.

Why invest in building relationships with existing customers when there is always another daft punter round the corner? Quality and service are an unnecessary expense if you don't care whether today's customer comes back tomorrow. Why put time and effort into staff training if you will be recruiting someone new shortly?

Why go to great lengths listening to and building up relations with difficult, unreasonably opinionated and demanding shareholders when it is easier to find new people willing to speculate and invest in you?

Strengths

If this was a car it would be perfect for driving down the King's Road, always painted black with blacked-out windows, huge chromed wheels, a shiny exhaust and a most impressive spoiler.

Weaknesses

Shallow and venal, this culture does not suit those with integrity. It does what it needs to do but if I owned one I would park it around the corner.

Overall verdict ★

This culture is about the here and now, and mortgaging the future. It believes in divide and rule within the leadership team, across functions and levels within the organization, and most definitely with suppliers, customers and investors.

Knowledge is power not to be willingly shared and everyone else is an adversary. The best way to confuse a believer in the exploitation culture is to ask him who is trying to screw him the most; his colleagues, his employees, his suppliers, his customers or his shareholders!

The exploitation culture has a slash and burn mentality that rapes the land today and then moves on to the next patch. It generates waste and endangers scarce resources.

In human relation terms it is scared of commitment, prone to infidelity, prefers a series of one-night stands to a serious relationship and thinks of marriage as an institution for fools. You have been warned!

The performance culture: leader-centric

Under the performance culture, short-termism is king! Process improvement, efficiency and systemization are seen as paramount. Financial manoeuvring and short-term share performance dominate board agendas.

The last 20 years have seen large amounts of business consultancy and business theory develop around the performance culture and, as a result, some current business advice now falls under the banner of 'fix it or spin it'!

Strengths

Sick and tired of airy-fairy nonsense? Then this is without doubt the solution for you. This culture calls a spade a spade and is not afraid of a little mess. The performance culture is a four-wheel drive off-roader – God help anything that gets in its way. Buy it complete with a full set of bull bars – pedestrians, cyclists and old people beware!

Weaknesses

When not being used as God intended, this culture will disappoint. Ride quality is poor and it is not fleet of foot, light to manoeuvre or easy to park.

Who needs a massive off-roader to get a newspaper?

This culture has a tendency to be loud, dominating and a bit of a bully prone to overconfidence in its abilities, believing that strength in one area equals strength in all areas.

If you wear your hiking boots at home sitting in front of the telly, then this is the one for you.

Overall verdict ★★

Godfather to downsizing, real-sizing, process re-engineering and time and motion studies, this one is a force to be reckoned with. It teaches that:

- people are only motivated by one thing and that is money – forget the other stuff and cut to the chase, how much does it cost?;

- customers don't want service or quality they won't pay for – customers and suppliers cannot be trusted and customer service is for wimps; and

- employee satisfaction is dangerous hokum – employees are basically lazy and need tight management. Pay good money, get the best, sack them after a month if they don't perform. Training is for losers.

Exponents of the performance culture are generally the best-informed. They deal extensively in tangibles with little account taken of intangibles such as employee and customer satisfaction.

Cost-cutting ideas are usually viewed as innocent until proven guilty, whilst other ideas are guilty until proven innocent.

Being the best-informed, however, doesn't make you right.

Devotees of the performance culture take advantage of the failure of businesses to measure and report on non-financial matters to override the views of other directors.

Their status as masters of the knowledge is further backed up by the regulatory and financial obligations on businesses to report on the things that the performance culture holds to be sacrosanct.

This wealth of information, together with the ability to avoid taking risks, gives rise to a high level of confidence amongst exponents of the performance culture. They always know the answer but it is invariably viewed from one perspective, which boils down to a victory of efficiency over effectiveness.

This produces a string of projects and initiatives where specific performance measures take on an importance way beyond their real value. Single-issue management, such as judging the performance of a hospital solely by the length of its waiting list, is a major risk.

There is obviously nothing wrong with tight financial management but that is not what we are talking about here. This is about directors manipulating reporting systems to ensure that they get large bonuses to the detriment of the whole organization.

Carried to extremes, the performance culture can be destructive, parasitic and pompous, eschewing risk and judging the failings of others.

In human terms it could be described as a pub bore with a view on the rights and wrongs of everything and everyone but not averse to buying a bit of knocked-off gear on the cheap.

Recognition culture: employee-centric

This is a bit of a hybrid culture that bears similarities with the performance culture but differs in one major respect.

Whereas money and self-interest are the prevailing influences in the performance culture, personal recognition is the goal here. Popular amongst those shielded from the full rigours of competition, the recognition of a job well done takes on great importance.

When an organization is so large that people stop seeing how their role makes a difference to the big picture, the respect of peers becomes very important. While working for BT during its heyday I witnessed internal recognition sometimes exert a greater influence on employee behaviour than even pay and promotion.

> "... when the pursuit of internal or external recognition becomes a goal in its own right it will distract an organization, waste energy and become divisive ..."

Strengths

Very much a culture that wants to be seen, this is the prestige end of the market – and who doesn't enjoy a bit of luxury from time to time?

Weaknesses

As with most luxuries, this does not come cheap. It can become obsessive when it takes over your life: let's face it, there must be more to life than work and keeping up with the Joneses.

Overall verdict ★★★

With people spending longer at work than they do at home, recognition counts. A person's whole self-esteem can rest on the company car they drive, whether their office has a meeting table or, in this day and age, whether they even have an office.

Organizational symbolism is powerful stuff and – however much it is politically correct to rubbish it and say that the trappings of success are wrong – used wisely, it can have a positive effect on both organizational performance and on individual well-being.

The ultimate demonstration of the recognition culture is the honours system and, regardless of the strengths and weaknesses of the current system, no one can deny its underlying power.

When the pursuit of internal or external recognition becomes a goal in its own right it will distract an organization, waste energy and become divisive. People in effect start using the organization's resources for their own ends.

There is nothing wrong however with endorsing desired behaviour and making people feel good about doing a good job through a timely, public thank you.

Rights culture: employee-centric

This culture tends to come about as a direct response to confrontation between the leaders of an organization and its employees. Often found in conjunction with profit, performance, institutional and exploitation cultures, it is the cost of cutting too many relationship corners.

When trust breaks down between the different parties in an organization, each party takes it upon themselves to defend their own position and to defend it as rigorously as possible.

This culture was at the height of its popularity during the 1970s when trade unions nearly brought the country to its knees. Arthur Scargill is probably lifetime president of the rights culture and personally represents its beliefs pretty well.

> "... very obvious to spot and very damaging in its most extreme forms, [the rights culture] is also extremely dangerous and costly in even its mildest incarnations ..."

Strengths

In motoring terms this is less a car and more of a bus, and like much public transport it is far from perfect; but if it is the only way to get from A to B, then it becomes attractive.

Weaknesses

Expect to wait a long time for one and then several will come along. Often noisy and slow, this is for many very much a culture of last resort.

Overall verdict ★

The rights culture is a cost of failure: the failure of an organization to develop mutually respectful relationships between managers and employees.

Very obvious to spot and very damaging in its most extreme forms, it is also extremely dangerous and costly in even its mildest incarnations.

The rights culture will be present in all organizations suffering from chronic corporate stress and will cost organizations significantly both monetarily and socially.

No-one can win when the rights culture is present: employees lose out and leaders lose out because the waste associated with organizations in Denial will always mean that at the end of the day there will be less cake to be shared by everyone. The rights culture and Corporate Denial go hand-in-hand and are extremely infectious, spreading like wildfire across an organization. If you even suspect that it might be present, act immediately.

It is also very good at hopping from one organization to another, so even if you just trade with an organization that you think may have the rights culture present, be very careful that it doesn't drag you down with it.

Independence culture: employee-centric

The independence culture is a natural successor to the rights culture and is partly a result of the Thatcher years and partly down to the popular reaction against relying on others for anything. Independence is now widely held up as a virtue and seems to be the ultimate goal for everyone over about 12 years old.

The perceived failure of many of the established institutions to provide a strong lead of any kind has added to the problem. If the Church, the government or the monarchy can't deliver any type of believable guidance, it falls onto the shoulders of individuals to fill the gap for themselves.

And if we were naive enough to expect much from so-called celebrities, we were in for another disappointment. When everybody from footballers and media stars through to senior corporate figures are seen to be out for all they can get with no sign of any public responsibility, ordinary people see no reason not to follow suit. Corporate fat cats and companies such as Enron have been the last nail in an already tightly closed coffin.

With independence now considered a higher virtue than service, people's first loyalty is often to themselves – even when they are still taking the 'King's shilling' and working within a large organization.

Under the independence culture people feel little necessity to go off on their own to be independent and are quite happy to sit tight, sod the rest of them and do their own thing where they are. If the chairman and CEO can do it, why can't they?

The introduction of home-working and hot-desking has added to this trend as well. With far greater personal freedom and reduced emotional bonds, why should anyone feel they must sell themselves to the company any more?

It would be interesting to know how many organizations have calculated the cost of lost loyalty associated with these new ideas.

They say that absence makes the heart grow fonder, but not in the case of home-working and hot-desking: here, absence makes the garden grow greener!

Strengths

If you want to have your cake and eat it this is the culture for you. This is the VW Beetle Cabriolet or Mini Cooper S Cabriolet of culture. Wind-in-the-hair motoring for those that just want to have fun and know how to have it.

Weaknesses

Few weaknesses are evident for able employees who will enjoy the freedom that comes with the independence culture, but in a less severe way than the rights culture this one is also a cost of failure in some respects.

Employers have taken the benefits of reduced costs and responsibilities for employees, and must now deal with the impact of reduced loyalty and weakened employee relations.

Overall verdict ★★★

The rise of the independence culture has coincided with a mass of books being published on the subject of being in charge of your own life. You name it and there is now a book about it: *Float Your Own Canoe*, *Paddle Your Own Boat*, *Be Your Own Personnel Director*, *Me Inc.* and so it goes on. Stick this lot on top of a whole pile of other self-help books and it is no wonder that people are helping themselves.

But this can become a problem for organizations if it is not managed.

Fewer organizations are now taking responsibility for the welfare of their staff and at the same time are increasingly implementing policies that reduce their influence and control.

Many organizations are not compensating for this more distant type of employee relationship with greater training or culture development programmes, and the personal behaviour of directors may also be at odds with the way that companies want their employees to behave. On top of this the length of time that people stay in jobs is decreasing and so loyalty to organizations is in danger of hitting an all-time low.

It is no wonder that organization-wide cultures are being replaced by cultures such as this!

This culture uses negotiation where the rights culture uses confrontation, but the result can still potentially be similar: a breakdown of trust and values amongst those within an organization and an increasing inability to deal consistently with customers.

The independence culture does not necessarily threaten success but it may threaten those who wish to go further and strive for amazing success. When money, cost and efficiency are the only things of importance in a relationship, it is time to be very concerned.

Service culture: customer-centric

The service culture is basically the Character Ethic for organizations.

It is built on the same basic principles of integrity, humility, fidelity, courage, justice, simplicity, modesty, the concept of service, the pursuit of excellent relationships and hard work.

The service culture places special values on the paramount importance of all relationships, especially customer service. Transparency, mutual respect, the vital role of communication, shared involvement and personal demonstration by the organization's leadership team are the fundamental principles.

Strengths

Where do you start with the service culture? It really is the business.

With the prestige of Mercedes, the sporting prowess of BMW, the technical expertise of Audi, the performance of Porsche, the style of Aston Martin, the flair of Ferrari, the audacity of Rolls-Royce, the practicality of a Volvo Estate and the strength of a Toyota Pickup, this is some culture.

Where can I buy one?

Weaknesses

This is a beautifully engineered culture, second to none for picking the kids up from school in, but ...

As with every working culture, it has its weaknesses. In this case, there are two obvious ones:

- it does not come cheap; and
- it has a long waiting list.

These are the reasons you don't see more service cultures about.

Being handmade has its drawbacks and for the service culture it means there are no short-cuts. You need the money to buy it and you need the money

to run it – if of course you have the patience to wait long enough to get one made especially to your specification.

Overall verdict ★★★★★

This is the culture of organizational connoisseurs.

As with all specialist items, however, it must be handled by a specialist to perform to its best.

If life at work was the one-dimensional stereotype that we read so much about, then I would be telling everyone to use this culture. But in the real world that would be nonsense.

- Adopting a service culture will kill some organizations.
- Adopting a service culture will severely harm others.

This culture is expensive and you can't make it work overnight. Use it for the wrong reasons and you will go broke.

Organizations are not people and they have to play by different rules. The Character Ethic may be the best for every person but the service culture doesn't suit every organization.

The service culture:

- only suits organizations with the resources, the opportunity and the will to build a long-term business;
- is perfect for avoiding corporate stress;
- is the culture of choice for those that choose to confront Corporate Denial;
- is not the only successful culture;
- must be handled with care;
- supports long-term relationships; and
- is the culture of choice for amazing success.

Profit culture: investor-centric

The most obvious contrast between a profit culture and a service culture is not so much profit versus service as short-term versus long-term. Those driven by a profit culture are extremely keen to see a good return on investment today and are usually unprepared to wait a bit longer for the boat to come in.

Typical of many stock market driven companies in the UK, there is little incentive for either investors or directors to put time and money into a future that they do not expect to feature in.

Stocks are traded so rapidly that long-term prospects are only important to the extent that they influence today's share price. Investors would rather sell today and buy back when shares are lower than take a hit investing for the future. With so many directors' benefits linked to share performance, who wants to stick their neck out?

"... this culture is a cop-out; it disregards human qualities and relationships, and probably delivers less ..."

Strengths
If you want to fit in you will like the profit culture: no-one gets fired for buying one of these.

Weaknesses
It makes almost any other culture look exciting. If it was a car it would be a cross between an ageing stretch limo and a Ford Granada.

I don't think this is a good culture. Yes, it is safe and reliable, but frankly, I would rather drive around in a hearse.

This culture is a cop-out; it disregards human qualities and relationships, and probably delivers less in the end as well.

Overall verdict ★★
This culture represents some of the worst of British business. It is the heartland of those that aspire to be OK and put innovation and risk-taking in the same camp as leprosy. Where the profit culture goes so does Corporate Denial, and it is not the exclusive domain of big business either.

Do you see those little signs next to traffic light saying 'Earn £500 a day in your spare time' or get letters telling you that you have won a million pounds and to call a number to claim your suitcase stuffed with cash?

Does the money arrive or do you end up calling the Cayman Islands on a premium number at £5 a minute?

Don't be seduced. I know immediate reward always sounds tempting, but like everything wickedly bad for us there is going to be a price to pay.

Partnership culture: community-centric

Here is a culture with a difference. The partnership culture is a complete cross between several other cultures.

Sharing values with both the service culture and the results culture, the partnership culture opens up the inner circle of stakeholders much wider than just investors.

The partnership culture puts the relationship emphasis on those involved in delivering the service in much the same way as the service culture values customers.

Strengths
This is a soundly based working culture that values the safety and comfort of its passengers very highly. This is the Volvo of cultures but with the added benefit of dual controls. Comfortable, capable and safe, this may suit particularly if you don't mind a driving school sign on your roof.

Weaknesses
It is hard to be very dynamic with so much advice and more than one person at the controls.

Overall verdict ★★★★
This is an underused and underpotentialized working culture. It has many of the advantages of some of the best in the market but somehow is still being held back; maybe it is not being very well marketed.

Unlikely to be the fastest, it should perform well in the long run if you balance the needs of the partners with the need for fleetness of foot, individual personality and rapid response to changing market conditions.

Philanthropy culture: community-centric

The philanthropy culture comes into force when more than money is at stake. This culture is the complete opposite of many of the others.

Both extremely short-term (a famine relief campaign, for example) through to extreme long-term (sustainability and save the planet), this culture can be very adaptable.

What matters in these organizations is that they must work harder than almost any others to unify their working culture. Everybody from trustees, hired professional managers, local volunteers to the general public needs a razor-sharp view of the organization's aims and where exactly the money is going to be spent.

> "... [this culture] can tap into a well of passion and support that is second to none ..."

Strengths

This is the VW Campervan of working cultures. Either beautifully restored in duck egg blue and cream or painted bright yellow and covered in flowers, it does not matter.

Weaknesses

This culture must avoid the trap of amateurism or too many mechanics trying to keep it on the road. How often do you see a well-presented Campervan on the hard shoulder surrounded by half a dozen surfer dudes desperate to get to the surf but sadly going nowhere?

Overall verdict ★★★

This is a culture with almost more potential than any other because it can tap into a well of passion and support that is second to none.

Far too often, however, I have seen it tied up in knots to the point that it is covered by a stultifying web of confusion that suffocates all relationships.

Because posts in philanthropic organizations are often voluntary and because the goal is not simply a clear-cut profit margin then true purpose is often open to interpretation and goes unmeasured. Although straightforward financial goals come with a myriad of downsides at least they provide an element of focus!

Philanthropic organizations or charities are often hotbeds of Denial because they are not crisp about their goals or even, surprisingly, their values.

The trustees or governors of many communities are, I am afraid to say, often completely out of their depth and cause no end of problems.

They have little idea of their responsibilities and are not held accountable for their actions save in the case of a life-threatening disaster. To add insult to injury they can also be highly opinionated and out of touch with the modern world. The appointment process is often shrouded in mystery, with those making the appointments choosing who they think would fit in best with the current team rather than assessing their ability to do the job! Those who have the audacity to ask if they might be involved are automatically seen as inappropriate.

This situation is a travesty and if you know a trust, school or charitable organization in this situation, it is beholden on you to try and sort it out.

My experience has taught me that philanthropic working cultures can respond amazingly well to the right treatment, with stress and Denial rapidly becoming a thing of the past.

They need complete clarity because they rely on complex relationships to be successful. But most of all they need someone bold enough to take them by the scruff of the neck and start the recovery process regardless of the resistance that seems to spring up in virtually every case of this kind.

Once there is real clarity the passion of those involved can be caught and unleashed on the general public with amazing success.

If there is a broken philanthropy culture near you then call me!

Overall results

So how do the different cultures stand up?

Culture	Overall score
Service culture	★★★★★
Results culture	★★★★
Partnership culture	★★★★
Brand culture	★★★
Recognition culture	★★★
Independence culture	★★★
Philanthropy culture	★★★
Institutional culture	★★
Performance culture	★★
Profit culture	★★
Exploitation culture	★
Rights culture	★

Not surprisingly the service culture earns a well-deserved lead – but don't overlook the merits of results and partnership cultures!

From Primitives to Mercenaries and beyond

There is not always a direct correlation between culture type and maturity of organization but there are certainly some strong links and associations.

Organizational type	Culture employed	Culture rating
Primitive	Results	★★★★
Mercenary	Independence	★★★
	Brand	★★★
	Recognition	★★★
	Performance	★★
Feudal	Institutional	★★
	Profit	★★
	Expolitation	★
	Rights	★
Advanced	Service	★★★★★

It is harder to recognize such clear connections in the case of either the partnership or philanthropy cultures.

In both these cases, the maturity of the organization is less dependent on the type of culture adopted and more dependent on the manner in which the culture is applied.

The reality of working cultures

The reality of working cultures is of course that you cannot buy them off-the-shelf and that they are as individual as each organization.

But this exercise does prove a number of things.

- When it comes to culture, the key issue is developing the right working culture for the organization and not simply that one culture type is right for every occasion.

- What makes or breaks a working culture is not the main thrusts but the nuances and shades, as well as the integrity with which it is applied.

- Almost every working culture, even the poorest-performing, can deliver success under the right conditions and for a certain length of time.

- It is impossible to unify a whole organization using some working cultures. The combative and unbalanced nature of the exploitation culture, profit culture, performance culture and institutional culture will almost inevitably encourage either the rights culture or the independence culture to take hold, leading to unavoidable loss of focus, damaged relationships and impaired performance.

- Organizations must be flexible enough to grow, develop and change their working cultures at appropriate times as size and market demand.

- High-performance cultures are harder and more expensive to maintain but deliver more consistent relationships.

- If an organization intends to go all the way to amazing success then it must overcome far greater challenges than those facing an averagely successful organization. It must demonstrate working values, corporate relationships and an organizational culture beyond the grasp of even many successful organizations, and it must be able to maintain these over time – even in the face of significant barriers and distractions.

The *What Culture?* Culture of the Year

Amazingly successful organizations must develop a working culture similar to the service culture described here.

Principles of Effective Relationships

wjm

The principles of effective relationships include:

Honesty and integrity

Truth, trust and peace are essential for effective relationships. You can fool some of the people some of the time but no organization can consistently fool all of the people all of the time.

Fairness

The concept of fairness is often overlooked in today's organizations but is as important today as ever. What goes around comes around and relationships that are not built around fairness cannot last.

Belief in the potential for growth

Hope is a cornerstone of Primitive Organizations but is squeezed out as organizations grow. Hope means far more than being optimistic about current market forecasts: it is a spirit capable of shaping a whole organization's attitude to relationships.

Patience

Amazing success does not happen overnight and effective relationships take time to build.

Encouragement and support for others

Coaching is an everyday act for those that naturally build great relationships. Any organization that neglects coaching and mentoring will miss out on many of the best aspects of growing and learning as a team. Good teams, like good families, rely on an extended network of both close and more distant contacts to strengthen and develop everyone.

Even the most senior members of a team need help and some would argue that the more senior we get, the more coaching we need to stay at our very best. You rarely find amazing sportsmen deciding they don't need a coach because they have just won a major title.

Courage

Courage is a prerequisite for anyone trying to confront Denial. When relationships need rebuilding, courage is what it takes to lay the first stone.

Humility and modesty

These are not big scorers with corporate fat cats – but then, they just want to take the money and run. Humility and modesty help you maintain strong relationships when times are good so that when times are not so good, you have friends to call on.

The pursuit of excellence

How good do you want to be?

- Is 'ordinary' enough?
- Is 'OK' OK?
- Is 'better than the others' good enough?
- Is 'good' great?
- Or do you want to be the very best you can be?

Highly effective relationships and striving for excellence go hand in hand!

Simplicity

Keep it simple: complications slow relationships down and get you caught in a web of intrigue you don't need.

Hard work and personal endeavour

There is no short-cut to amazing success and amazing relationships; hard work is as essential now as it has ever been.

The concept of service

Of all the virtues on this list the concept of service is probably one of the most fundamental.

If we view relationships purely as a resource to be exploited, that is what they will become. They will be transactional and no goodwill or trust will be built up. They will serve their immediate purpose but not become the pillars of strength that are needed to deliver amazing success.

Service is now considered to be old-fashioned and rather quaint. The idea of devoting oneself to service of any kind – be it to a country, an organization, a religion or indeed anything – is in fact openly derided by some.

In many organizations service and servitude have unfortunately become intrinsically linked. Being involved in delivering service is looked down on as somehow an inferior profession, so people no longer take personal pride in delivering great service.

But there is a cost to this and that cost is paid in damaged and broken relationships.

Communicating openly

Communication is the last but by no means least important facet of effective relationships. If the average organization quadrupled its levels of internal communication and doubled external communication, it might start to get close to where it needs to be.

I regularly work with organizations that ignore whole chunks of their relationship base and as a result of these relationship blind spots, they end up with crippled relationships.

Example Truth Map Questions

wjm

Truth Map questions

Clearly the exact questions asked within any Truth Map must relate specifically to the organization being audited, but there are some basic questions that
we can start with.

The audience groups that we address usually include the:

- leadership team;
- management group;
- employees;
- market place – customers and suppliers;
- shareholders and other stakeholders; and
- community and environment.

Template questions asked include:

Purpose and direction

- What exactly is the organization trying to achieve?
- How widely agreed is this amongst managers?
- How well understood is this across the whole organization?
- What makes you think these opportunities are real?
- Is this attractive to investors?
- Does this impact on society or the environment?

Leadership and communication

- Does the leadership team personally demonstrate what it preaches and
  does it communicate effectively?
- How effective is the management team at converting the organization's
  leadership into everyday policy and guidance?
- Are the organization's leaders respected across the entire organization?
- Does the market place recognize the strength and value of the organization's leadership?
- How much value do investors place on the quality of the leadership
  team?

Performance and innovation

- Is the leadership team recognized as being personally well-organized and open to questioning?
- How well do you respond to opportunities whilst minimizing waste?
- Have you established effective delegation and authority to act across the organization?
- Is the organization focused on customer needs?
- What benchmarks exist to validate and measure performance and innovation?

Teamwork and culture

- Is the leadership team transparent and involving?
- Is there a culture of innovation and personal responsibility?
- Do people feel that their contribution is recognized and valued?
- Do customers ever get the benefit of good organizational teamwork?
- What value do investors put on the equality of the organization's teamwork?
- How much respect are relationships treated with?

Products and services

- How often does the entire leadership team talk to customers about what they want?
- Are you clear about what you sell, who buys it and why?
- Does everyone understand this and how their personal role fits the bigger picture?
- Do customers see the relevance to them?
- How different do investors think you are from your competitors? (Do they have all the facts they need to know?)
- Are there any environmental issues to think about?

Customer service, sales and client management

- Does the leadership team stay in touch with the people that serve customers?
- How do you measure customer satisfaction and manage client opportunities?

- Is everyone focused on meeting customer needs?
- How satisfied are customers?
- Can you value the full extent of the goodwill within your organization?

Identity, look and feel

- Does the leadership team understand and personally take responsibility for the impact of corporate identity?
- Do all aspects of your identity tell the same story?
- Does your visual expression reflect your aspirations?
- Are your internal and external communication policies understood and adhered to?
- Do customers and potential customers relate to and value your existing communication? How do you know?
- How much is your brand worth and what could be done to raise its value?

Information and knowledge

- How well informed is the leadership team?
- Is communication regular and is information freely shared?
- Does everyone have the information they need to do their job properly?
- Do customers and potential customers receive all the information they need?
- How well do you communicate with and involve investors?
- Is it a learning organization?

The Contributing Team

Will Murray

wjm Business Relationships

Will is now firmly established as a leading organizational coach, relationship troubleshooter, business writer and commentator on relationship issues.

Will works with an amazing array of organizations from small businesses, trusts, public sector organizations to major PLCs.

In the vanguard of those who recognize that organizations stand or fall not on the strength of their processes but on the strength of their relationships, Will is leading the way in applying Truth and Reconciliation in Business and in the art of Relationship Mapping.

With no organizational relationship too big or too small, Will is now a regular speaker on the subject of Amazing Relationships versus Corporate Denial.

Will is also the author of *Brand Storm*, published by Financial Times Prentice Hall, and *Hey You!*, published by Momentum.

will@willjmurray.com

Annalese Banbury

The Business Brief: purpose, focus, communication

As a founding partner of The Business Brief, Annalese is an expert at relationship management and the interaction between leadership teams and their organizations.

Annalese is often required to champion the importance of relationships to the continuing success of an organization, particularly when she is the sole female representative within the change team. Heavily relied upon for her coaching skills, Annalese guides organizations through the turbulent and uncharted waters of culture change.

annalese@thebusinessbrief.com

Tim Guy

tgd: business-focused communication

Timing is everything and Tim was lucky to be in at the beginning of the UK's resurgence in graphic design in the 1960s.

By the time Tim opened his practice in Richmond, he had learnt the printing trade in Cambridge, been through the new London College of Printing's Art & Design degree course and toured around Scandinavia care of an RSA bursary award.

Taught by FHK Henrion, he developed a multi-disciplinary design business tackling interior design projects with the same enthusiasm devoted to developing packaging solutions for the Queen's dog food suppliers.

Today, Tim runs a business-focused communications consultancy with the same attitude and confidence that has served him well for 34 years in the design and communications industry.

The backbone of Tim's business remains a commitment to loyal service and the business relationships that have served him well for a third of a century.

timguy@tgd.co.uk

David Birt

db&co: direction for communication design

David has over 20 years' experience, leading diverse and challenging design and communications projects for some of the world's best-known companies.

As the co-developer of Message Mapping with Tim Guy, David is guided by two fundamental principles:

- great communication design should clearly and evidentially link with strategic business objectives; and
- great business relationships are essential to making communication solutions work.

db&co provide solutions for companies who want compelling, precise, relevant, insightful and proven communication design for their investors, business customers, consumers or employees.

David previously held key positions in leading strategic design companies Conran Design Group and tgd.

davidbirt@dbandco.co.uk

Lauris Calnan

bcg: market research services

With over 20 years' market research and brand experience with Reed Business Information PLC, several B2B advertising agencies and McKinsey Management Consultants, Lauris has been responsible for several large international project-management initiatives.

In 1992 Lauris was one of the founding directors of the Bingham Calnan Group of companies, which provide brand research and consultancy advice to large organizations.

Lauris is also a guest speaker and lecturer at a number of international business conferences on the subject of corporate brand development.

lauris@binghamcalnan.com

Between us we have worked with:

AstraZeneca, BA, BHS, Blue Circle, BT, Buckingham Palace, the Burton Group, Conran, Corus PLC, the Dixons Group, Druid PLC, Ernst & Young, Exeter University, Fujitsu, GE, GlaxoWellcome, House of Fraser, HP, Innogy, Insead, Lotus Notes, the National Express Group, Microsoft UK, the National Grid, the Open University, Orange, The Royal Collection, Société Générale, St Paul's Cathedral, Tetley, Thorn EMI, Truro High School, Victrex, Virgin Records, Xansa, and Yell, amongst others ...

Index